Bankers' Services and Lending Handbook

Bankers' Services and Lending Handbook

Geoffrey Sales, ACIB
Peter Ibbetson, ACIB

The Chartered Institute of Bankers

First published 1990

BANKERS BOOKS LIMITED
c/o The Chartered Institute of Bankers
10 Lombard Street
London EC3V 9AS

Chartered Institute of Bankers (CIB) Publications are published by Bankers Books Limited under an exclusive licence and royalty agreement. Bankers Books Limited is a company owned by The Chartered Institute of Bankers.

ISBN 0 85297 260 1

🄑🄛   British Library Cataloguing in Publication Data

Sales, Geoffrey
  Bankers' Services and Lending Handbook
  1. Great Britain. Banks. Customer Services
  I. Title. II. Ibbetson, Peter
  1956–
  332.10941

Typeset 10/12pt Times, by Cotswold Typesetting Ltd, Cheltenham
Printed by Commercial Colour Press Ltd, London E7.
Text on 80gsm woodfree; cover on 240gsm matt coated artboard, one-sided.

Contents

Contents

Foreword

The Chartered Institute of Bankers commissioned two experienced lecturers, Geoffrey Sales and Peter Ibbetson, both Associates of the Institute, to write a handbook for students of *Practice of Banking 2*, the examination which will become the Stage 2 retail banking option, *Branch Banking—Lending and Marketing*. It is designed to assist not only students but also practitioners by providing a convenient reference point for day-to-day problem solving.

The authors have vast banking and teaching experience. Both have served for many years as examiners, and have conducted revision courses for the Institute. The combined experience of the authors undoubtedly provides an invaluable handbook for today's branch banker.

Justyn Young FCIB
Assistant Secretary
The Chartered Institute of Bankers

PART A   ADVANCES

1 | Principles of Lending to Personal Customers

Overview

There are several mnemonics for remembering the principles of lending, the idea being that they serve as guidelines or as a checklist for remembering the key features of *any* lending proposition. The mnemonic used here is PARTS—purpose, amount, repayment, term, security—plus personal characteristics.

Purpose

Almost any purpose is acceptable so long as it is legal.

Two areas inherently involve extra risk and may be viewed less enthusiastically than others:

(a) Speculation, e.g., 'stagging' new share issues.
(b) Consolidation of debts owed to other lenders.

However, even these may be acceptable if the rest of the features in the proposition are sound.

Amount

Is it enough?

Is the Customer making a contribution?

Banks can lend 100% but a contribution is preferred and usually insisted upon.

Repayment

What is the cost of the borrowing to the customer?

Calculate interest and capital repayments to arrive at the monthly repayment figure.

Can the customer meet the monthly repayment figure from net income?

Examine the customer's monthly income and expenditure budget (including loan repayment).

Considerations which will affect budget:

(a)   Is a rise in income due shortly?

(b)   Is there evidence of regular savings with other institutions which could be used to repay loan, e.g., standing order to building society or to a savings plan.

(c)   Are there any regular commitments due to expire, e.g., hire-purchase agreement?

(d)   Don't overlook 'cash' expenses, e.g., food, clothing, petrol, entertainment. These are never given in a question but a realistic assessment will have to be made.

Term

Different banks have different 'rules'.

Flexible up to five years but:

(a)   Second-hand cars—maximum two years.
(b)   property extensions or improvements could be up to 10 years.
(c)   household goods—maximum three years.

These are general guidelines not fixed rules.

The term will be influenced by the customer's ability to repay.

Security

Personal loans are usually unsecured.

Personal characteristics

Character

What does the bank know about the customer?

Is the customer trustworthy?

Can the bank rely on the customer's word?

Connection

How long has the bank known the customer?

Is the customer involved in other accounts, e.g., as a director of a company?

Is the customer a useful source of business and contacts, e.g., a solicitor, accountant etc.

Past record

Has the customer borrowed previously?

If so, was the borrowing repaid in accordance with agreement or did the bank have difficulty in recovering the debt?

Has the customer's current account been conducted satisfactorily?

Other factors

The bank will cross-sell any other services which are relevant to the circumstances, e.g., sickness insurance.

Personal loans in examinations

Personal loan lending for consumer goods purchases is a rare examination topic, presumably because in practice most of it is subject to credit scoring.

However the basic principles of lending will apply to any specialist type of personal lending (e.g., mortgage or bridging advance) and therefore serve as a useful guide.

2 | Bridging Finance

Overview

Any short-term advance which will be repaid from an identifiable and certain source of funds can be referred to as a 'bridge'. It is the gap in time which is being bridged, between having to make a payment and the receipt of funds. Bridging finance is most commonly found in change of property situations, where a customer is moving house and needs to purchase the new property before having sold the existing one.

A bridging advance can be either:

(a)   closed—where contracts have been exchanged for the sale of the existing house and a completion date is known—or

(b)   open-ended—where contracts on the existing house have not been exchanged and the period for which finance is required is not, therefore, known.

Purpose

Is it a closed bridge? If so, the term of the advance will be known and interest can be accurately calculated.

Is it open-ended? If so, there is no firm date for sale of the existing house, and interest cannot therefore be quantified.

The bank will be reluctant to lend in an open-ended situation unless there is a good margin and/or the customer has adequate liquid resources to meet interest for (say) up to 12 months.

Amount

The bank needs the following information in order to calculate the borrowing requirement:

(a)   Information about the purchase:

(i)   Price of house being purchased.

(ii)   Amount of mortgage arranged. Evidence will be required in the form of a letter of intent from the lender.

(iii)   Is the availability of the mortgage dependent on repayment of the mortgage on the house being sold and upon the result of a satisfactory survey?

(iv)   Has the deposit been paid or will this be included in the amount of the bridge?

(b)   Information about the sale.

(i)   Price of house being sold. Have contracts been exchanged? If not, is the bank satisfied that the asking price is realistic? Will the price have to be reduced and what is the lowest acceptable figure? Has the bank viewed the property?

(ii)   Amount of mortgage outstanding. Confirmation of this figure will be required.

Example 2.1

	£
Buying for	81,000
Mortgage arranged	60,000
Balance required	21,000
Selling for	35,000
Outstanding mortgage	11,000
Surplus	24,000

(a)   (i)   The availabilty of the new mortgage of £60,000 might be dependent on the existing mortgage being paid off. This is likely where the same lender is involved in both mortgages.

(ii)   In this situation, the customer is likely to ask for £81,000, i.e., the full purchase price.

(iii)   The customer does not really need £81,000. The only obstacle to the new mortgage of £60,000 being made available is the existence of the old mortgage of £11,000.

(iv)   Therefore, the bank lends £11,000 to clear the existing mortgage. The new mortgage then becomes available, leaving a further £21,000 needed to complete the purchase. Total bridging advance £32,000.

(b)   This example assumes that the 10% deposit is to be included in the bridging advance.

(c)   (i)   If the new mortgage of £60,000 was being obtained from a different lender to the one who advanced the mortgage of £11,000, then the availability of the new mortgage would not be dependent on the existing one being repaid.

(ii)   In that case, the customer would need a bridge of only £21,000 to complete the purchase.

Repayment

The source of repayment is the sale proceeds of the existing house.

Will there be sufficient margin to repay the advance plus interest? The following factors will affect the margin:

(a)   Repayment of outstanding mortgage on existing house (unless the bank has already redeemed it as part of the bridging advance).

(b)   Failure to obtain the original asking price for the existing property (this will apply only to open-ended bridges). Will there still be sufficient margin if the asking price is reduced by 10%?

(c)   The costs involved:

(i)   Estate agents's fees on the house being sold. Say 2% of selling price.

(ii)   Stamp duty of 1% on price of house being purchased. This applies only where the price is in excess of £30,000, e.g.:

> Price £30,000:   stamp duty nil
> Price £30,500:   stamp duty £305

(iii)   Solicitor's fees. No fixed scale, depends on complexity of work done. Say £750.

(iv)   Removal expenses. Depends on distance travelled and insurance value of contents. Say £500.

(v)   Incidental expenses, such as new curtains, fixtures and fittings. Say £1,000.

(vi)   Interest on bridging advance. This is particularly important where the bridge is open-ended, but the amount will not be known. It would be prudent to allow for 12 months' interest.

If there is a shortfall in the margin, the bank may still lend if any of the following points apply:

(a)   The customer has sufficient liquid resources to cover the shortfall.

(b) The costs are being covered by someone else, e.g., the customer's employer, in which case confirmation should be sought.

(c) The customer is of sufficient standing for the bank to place the shortfall on a loan account to be repaid by instalments over an agreed period.

Example 2.2

Using the figures from example 2.1, the source of repayment is as follows:

(a) Bridge of £32,000 (where the bank has paid off the existing mortgage of £11,000 and advanced the balance of the purchase price, i.e., £21,000): the full sale proceeds of £35,000 of the existing house will be available because the mortgage has been redeemed. This leaves a margin of only £3,000.

(b) Bridge of £21,000 (where the balance of the purchase price had been advanced, i.e., it was not necessary to redeem the existing mortgage): the sale proceeds less the outstanding mortgage will be available, i.e., £24,000. Again, a margin of £3,000 is left.

A margin of £3,000 is small to meet all the costs, and the bank will be reluctant to lend (especially open-ended) unless one of the three ways of meeting a shortfall is applicable.

Term

Short term but depends on type of bridge.

If open-ended, the bank will need to be satisfied that there is good demand for the type of house being sold by the customer, and that the asking price is realistic. Both factors will affect the time-scale for a sale. A report on saleability is essential.

Security

In a closed-bridge situation, the bank may be prepared to rely on a solicitor's undertaking in respect of the sale proceeds.

Status enquiry will be made on solicitor, if not known.

In an open-ended bridge, the bank might take a charge over both properties or just the one being sold, depending on the circumstances.

Other factors

Interest rate will be in the region of 4% over base rate.

Bank will charge a commitment fee of (say) 1% of the amount lent, with a maximum of (say) £250–£300.

Selling opportunities:

(a)   Buildings and contents insurance.
(b)   Providing the mortgage on the property being purchased, if it is not already arranged.

3 | Home Loans

Overview

Mortgage lending forms a significant part of a bank's business. There are three main types of mortgage available:

(a) Repayment mortgage. The customer's monthly instalments cover both capital and interest. Mortgage protection life cover will be needed preferably for both parties where a joint purchase is involved.

(b) Endowment mortgage. The customer's monthly instalments cover interest only. The customer pays monthly premiums on an endowment policy which is used to repay the capital at the end of the term of the mortgage.

(c) Pension-linked mortgage. The customer's monthly instalments cover interest only. The customer makes monthly contributions to a pension fund, the cash portion of which is used at maturity to repay the capital sum of the mortgage.

Purpose

Usually available only for owner-occupied properties but some schemes are available for other properties.

Amount

A professional valuation of the property will be required.

The maximum amount available will be determined by:

(a) The lower figure of cost or professional valuation.

(b) The percentage of (a) which the bank is prepared to lend—usually 90% but can be less for higher value properties.

(c) Income(s) of borrower(s)—bank will apply its own multiplier, e.g., 3 times main income plus 1 times other income.

11

Example of multiplier

$$
\begin{array}{r}
£ \\
\text{X earns } £15,000 \times 3 = 45,000 \\
\text{Y earns } £10,000 \times 1 = \underline{10,000} \\
\underline{55,000}
\end{array}
$$

The maximum mortgage available would be £55,000. However, the main factor in determining the size of the loan is the ability of the customers to service the borrowing. A home loan of £55,000 would not be granted to X and Y, if it was obvious that they could not meet the repayments.

Repayment

Calculate monthly cost of borrowing.

Monthly commitment will include (where relevant) interest, capital, premiums on insurance policies, contributions to pension scheme.

Has allowance been made for the possible increase in monthly household expenditure, e.g., rates, lighting, heating, insurance etc.

Has allowance been made for legal fees etc?

Can monthly cost of home loan be serviced?

The bank will examine carefully the customer's budget for monthly income and expenditure.

For self-employed customers, accounts for the past two or three years will be required to show reliable level of income.

Term

Up to 25 years (may be longer in some instances).

For such long-term lending, it is important that the customer should be in reasonably stable employment, preferably with good prospects.

Security

First legal charge on the property being purchased.

Assignment of endowment policy (where relevant).

Mortgage indemnity insurance if lending more than 80%.

Other factors

The usual personal influences of character, connection, past record will apply.

Bank can cross-sell buildings and contents insurance plus (where relevant) mortgage protection insurance, endowment, pensions.

Cost of borrowing

Mortgage rates tend to be fairly volatile, e.g., during the course of a 12-month period the monthly repayment of a £60,000 mortgage might vary by as much as £100.

In practice, it is safer to look at a rate which is higher than the current rate, to see if the customer could service the loan if rates increased.

4 | Principles of Lending to Business Customers

Overview

The comments which follow are general in nature and will have to be adapted to the specific borrowing purpose and to the type of customer.

Purpose

Is it for working capital or for purchase of fixed assets?

What effect will it have on the balance sheet figures and ratios?

Will the purpose generate extra income or save on costs? This will affect repayment prospects, for example:

(a) Bank finance for a new contract will increase income.
(b) Bank finance to purchase existing premises at present being rented will not increase income but might reduce costs.

Amount

How does the amount compare with the net worth of the business?

Net worth could be boosted by any hidden reserves in the assets, e.g., freehold premises shown at cost.

The bank will not usually want to lend more than net worth (exceptions are mentioned in notes on specific lending situations).

For limited companies, assess the effect borrowing will have on the company's debt/equity ratio.

Evidence of amount will be required, e.g., cash-flow forecast to support overdraft request; estimates, costings, valuations for other purposes.

Equity or debt?

Traditionally banks prefer the customer to have a bigger stake in the business than the bank has. It is not unreasonable to expect the customer to take the bigger risk when it is the customer who will benefit more when the business does well.

It is always difficult to assess what is the right balance between debt and equity. Interest has to be paid on borrowed money irrespective of whether profits are made.

Heavily borrowed businesses will be particularly vulnerable to rises in interest rates.

Banks will be wary of highly geared businesses, i.e., a high level of debt in relation to equity, but it will not be so important in propositions where the purpose of the lending will generate funds to repay the advance fully, e.g., building advances.

Repayment

Calculate the cost of borrowing on an annual basis:

(a)   Interest on an estimated average balance for overdraft.
(b)   Interest and capital repayments for term loan.

Can the business service borrowing from its profits?

(a)   Examine profit retention record from financial information available (remember to add back depreciation and adjust for non-recurring items).
(b)   Can a profit forecast be drawn up from information given?

What prospects does the business have? What trends are seen in profitability in the accounts?

Sometimes repayment comes from an identifiable source not from normal trading profits, e.g., advances to builders are repaid from sale proceeds of houses.

Supporting information

In practice, banks will usually expect borrowers to produce cash-flow forecasts, budgets of sales, costs and profits, and in relevant cases such things as a break-even analysis and a capital investment appraisal.

In the examination, candidates might be expected to draw up a profit budget or break-even analysis, either from information given or based on previous results. If any forecast is given in a question then it will need to be commented on.

Term

Overdrafts reviewed annually or more frequently.

Loans up to 20 years depending on purpose and ability to repay.

Security

What is available?

(a) Sole traders and partners often have to charge their own property not used in the business, e.g., charge over house.

(b) Limited companies usually have more assets capable of being charged, e.g., charge over factory; debenture incorporating fixed charge over premises (and perhaps over plant and machinery) and book debts, with a floating charge over other assets. Directors' guarantees are often required.

Other factors

How long has the business been in existence? Is it well established or is it newly formed and developing?

How long has the business had an account with the bank?

How well does the bank know the people running the business? Are they reliable and trustworthy personally? Are they capable professionally? Can the bank rely on their projections?

What other information is available from the accounts? Ensure auditor's certificate is not qualified.

Key-man insurance will be necessary.

What trends are seen in liquidity and sales (as well as profitability)?

How well are credit and stock controlled?

Opportunities to cross-sell asset insurance; other forms of finance such as hire-purchase, leasing, factoring, pensions; will-appointments with personal tax and estate planning.

Management

In any business, the quality of the people who run it is a vital consideration:

(a) Personal details: age, health.

(b) Technical expertise: do they have the necessary technical knowledge or do they rely on other people? Do they have a relevant professional qualification?

(c) Financial expertise: is there someone in the management team who can produce the necessary supporting information or is it left to their accountant? Is there someone to apply the necessary control systems?

(d) Commitment: are they tied in financially, e.g., by guarantee?

(e) Is there a good spread of expertise?

(f) Is control evenly spread or is it in effect a 'one-man band'?

5 | Accounting Ratios

Overview

Accounting ratios will be provided in an examination question and these must be commented upon. The notes which follow give a few *broad* alternative interpretations, but candidates in the examination will have to provide precise interpretations relevant to the circumstances of the question.

Current ratio

An improving current ratio suggests:

(a) Profits being made.
(b) Sale of fixed assets.
(c) Borrowing being switched to medium term.

A deteriorating ratio suggests:

(a) Losses being made.
(b) Purchase of fixed assets.

Liquidity ratio

The liquidity ratio will usually follow the same pattern as the current ratio for the same reasons. However, the current ratio can show an improvement whilst the liquidity ratio deteriorates. This will reflect a build-up of stock, i.e., stock will be constituting a larger proportion of current assets than in previous years. Obviously the reverse is also true.

Debtors

An increasing number of days suggests:

(a) Less efficient debt collection.
(b) Potential bad debts—age list of debtors will show.
(c) Deliberate granting of longer credit to boost sales.

A decreasing number of days suggests:

(a)   More efficient debt collection—is this because the business experienced cash-flow problems?
(b)   Discounts being offerred for prompt payment.
(c)   A higher proportion of cash sales.

List of debtors

The bank overdraft is often used to finance debtors, i.e., the business needs cash for day-to-day operations but does not have sufficient because it has given credit to its customers. The situation is acceptable to the bank so long as it is certain that the debtors will pay on the due date. The later debtors pay, the greater is the liquidity problem.

A bigger problem occurs if a debt is bad. A large bad debt can wipe out a business's profit for that year. The bank needs to be able to assess that danger and will ask for an age list of debtors. This list serves two purposes:

(a)   It shows the spread of debts, i.e., evenly spread or heavy reliance on certain debtors.
(b)   It shows how long each debt has been outstanding—a debt which has remained unpaid for a long period is potentially bad.

Creditors

An increasing number of days suggests:

(a)   Longer credit being taken due probably to cash-flow problems. Are the creditors likely to apply any pressure? How much is owing to preferential creditors (important if the bank is either unsecured or relying heavily on a floating charge)?
(b)   Better credit terms arranged with suppliers.

A decreasing number of days suggests:

(a)   More prompt payment. Is this due to pressure by creditors or is it to take advantage of discounts being offered?
(b)   Suppliers enforcing less favourable credit terms.

There is a close relationship between credit given, credit taken and the operation of the bank account. If a business gives longer credit than it takes, then it will have a greater need for bank finance. Obviously the reverse is true.

Composition of creditors

The bank will prefer the creditors of a business to be evenly spread and might ask for a list to see what the situation is. Large creditors could cause problems if they started to press for payment.

In a liquidation, preferential creditors such as the Inland Revenue would have priority for payment of debts due to them over unsecured creditors and holders of a floating charge. Unless the bank is adequately secured by a legal charge on the business premises or a fixed charge over book debts, it will want to know the amount owing to preferential creditors.

Stock

An increasing number of days suggests:

(a) Stock turning over more slowly. Is some of the stock unsaleable? Might it have to be sold at a heavily discounted price?

(b) Excessive stocks due to poor stock control.

A decreasing number of stock days suggests:

(a) Stock turning over more quickly—therefore no obsolete stock.

(b) Stock levels too low—unable to carry stock at previous levels due to cash-flow problems.

Stock levels also affect bank borrowing. Excessive levels of stock tie up cash. Obsolete, unsaleable stock might result in increased overdraft and will distort gross profit figure upwards.

Gross profit

The major influence on gross profit margins are:

(a) Competition. An increase in the cost of supplies but the selling price to customers cannot be increased without losing business.

(b) An increase in fixed costs. This applies to manufacturers who might have an element of fixed costs in their production, e.g., factory rent.

(c) Changes in volume of sales of goods with different gross margins. Shopkeepers, for example, have different mark-ups on different items. If item X has a 20% gross margin and item Y a 10% margin, a large increase in volume of sales of item X will increase the overall gross margin of the business.

Net profit

The two factors which affect net profit are the level of gross profit and overheads. If everything is expressed as a percentage of sales, it becomes obvious.

	Year 1 £		Year 2 £		Year 3 £	
Sales	100,000		200,000		300,000	
Gross profit	30,000	(30%)	60,000	(30%)	120,000	(40%)
Overheads	20,00	(20%)	50,000	(25%)	75,000	(25%)
Net profit	10,000	(10%)	10,000	(5%)	45,000	(15%)

In year 2

    (a) Gross profit percentage remains the same.
    (b) Overheads as a percentage of sales rises.
    (c) Therefore, net profit percentage falls.

In year 3

    (a) Gross profit percentage rises.
    (b) Overheads as a percentage of sales remains constant.
    (c) Therefore net profit percentage rises.

6 | Financial Statements

Management accounts

Banks often grant facilities, especially where a debenture is held, on the condition that quarterly or monthly figures are produced for current assets and liabilities.

A depletion of net current assets is an early warning signal of losses being made (although it could also mean that fixed assets have been purchased).

Obviously an improvement in net current assets will mean profits (or exceptionally a sale of fixed assets).

If one of the dates for producing management accounts coincides with the balance sheet date, the bank will check the accuracy of the management figures against the balance sheet.

Funds flow statement

In practice a full statement of source and application of funds might be required.

A short form of funds flow statement is sufficient for the examination as follows:

Retained profit	X
Plus depreciation	Y
	Z

Purchase of fixed asssets	A
Increase/decrease in working capital	B
	Z

Any exceptional items such as the introduction of capital or sale of fixed assets will need to be included.

Estimated balance sheet

You will be expected to understand how proposed lending will affect the structure of the balance sheet (but not necessarily to draw one up).

Which parts of the balance sheet will be affected?

(a) Lending for working capital will affect current assets and current liabilities. For example:

(i) An overdraft to buy stock will increase current assets and current liabilities.

(ii) An overdraft to pay creditors will not affect the balance sheet. The bank overdraft will increase and creditors will decrease, i.e., one current liability is being transferred to another current liability.

(b) Lending to buy fixed assets will affect current liabilities and fixed assets. For example:

(i) A loan to buy plant and machinery will increase current liabilities and increase fixed assets. (Sometimes the major part of a loan is shown as a medium-term liability.)

You will be expected to understand how proposed lending will affect the gearing of the business, i.e., will increase debt of business thus bringing about a worsening of the debt/equity ratio.

Break-even analysis

This technique calculates the level of sales needed in order for a business to break even.

It is especially useful when assessing the viability of a new venture, e.g.:

Selling price   £5 per unit
Buying price   £3 per unit (variable cost)
Fixed costs   £20,000

(a) How many units have to be sold in order to cover fixed costs (i.e., break even)?
(b) Each unit contributes £2 (£5 − £3) to fixed costs.
(c) Therefore 10,000 units have to be sold to break even (10,000 × £2 = £20,000).
(d) Therefore break-even *sales* are £50,000 (10,000 × £5).

(e) The bank can now assess whether it thinks the business is capable of achieving sales of £50,000.

The technique is also useful where a business is making losses, i.e., to determine the level of sales needed in order to break even.

Example 6.1 Management accounts

	July (£000's)	August (£000's)	September (£000's)	October (£000's)
Debtors	86	90	97	101
Stock	59	56	63	66
	145	146	160	167
Creditors	63	58	63	70
Bank	41	42	45	43
	104	100	108	113
Sales	69	76	75	82

These figures show the following:

(a) A surplus of current assets over current liabilities, which is increasing. The increase is steady which should reflect profitable trading. If an asset has been sold, there would have been a big increase in that particular month (probably reflected in a reduction in 'bank').

(b) Credit given is:

$$\frac{\text{average debtors (93)}}{\text{sales (302)}} \times \text{period (123 days)} = 38 \text{ days}$$

How does this compare with credit given periods revealed in previous years' balance sheets?

It is important to be consistent in the way that the figures are compiled. The October debtors figure of 101 could have been used, which would have given 41 days, although average figures tend to be used more and more.

(c) Credit taken is:

$$\frac{\text{average creditors (63)}}{\text{sales (302)}} \times \text{period (123 days)} = 26 \text{ days}$$

How does this compare with previous figures? It would be more accurate to use cost of goods sold rather than sales, but consistency is essential for the comparison to be meaningful.

Note

In practice, it is likely that much more detailed information can be provided by businesses with their own computer facilities, e.g., end-of-month balance sheet, trading and profit statements, source and application of funds.

Example 6.2 Funds flow statement

EXTRACT FROM AUDITED ACCOUNTS

	Year A (£000's)	Year B (£000's)
Retained profit	20	23
Depreciation	14	16
Fixed assets	89	97
Net current assets	38	53

FUNDS FLOW STATEMENT FOR YEAR B

	(£000's)	
Retained profit	23	
Depreciation	16	
	39	
Purchase of fixed assets	24	(see below)
Increase in working capital	15	(53 minus 38)
	39	

The figure for fixed assets has increased by £8,000 but this is *after* depreciation of £16,000. Therefore there must have been an investment in fixed assets of at least £24,000, ignoring any sales of assets.

Example 6.3 Estimated balance sheet

Current assets	£200,000
Current liabilities	£100,000
	Ratio 2:1

Effect of advancing £50,000:
(1) To buy stock.
(2) To pay creditors.
(3) To buy machinery.

(1) Current assets   200+50=250
     Current liabilities   100+50=150

                                                  Ratio 1.7:1

(2) Current assets   200+Nil=200
     Current liabilities   100+Nil=100

                                                  Ratio 2:1

(3) Current assets   200+Nil=200
     Current liabilities   100+50 =150

                                                  Ratio 1.3:1

Note

Variations can be seen in the treatment of medium-term loans by bankers:

(a) Regarding them totally as current liabilities on the basis that they became due should any instalment be missed.

(b) Regarding them totally as a medium-term facility, and therefore omitting them from the current ratio.

(c) Regarding part as a current liability and part as medium term, e.g., 1/10th of a 10-year loan as being current.

Example 6.4 Break-even analysis

Figures extracted from latest audited accounts:

	£	
Sales	300,000	
Gross profit	15,000	(5%)
Overheads	22,000	(regard as fixed costs)
Net loss	(7,000)	

What is the level of break-even sales when it is expected that overheads will rise to £30,000 and gross margin will remain at 5%?

(a) Gross profit has to be £30,000 in order to cover overheads.

(b) Gross profit is 5% of sales.

(c) Sales have to be:

$$£30,000 \times \frac{100}{5} = £600,000$$

7 | Financing Working Capital

Overview

Ideally, an overdraft for working capital purposes should be used to smooth out timing differences between payments out and receipt of funds.

Businesses which have to sell on credit terms to customers will have a greater need for an overdraft, as they await payment from their customers, than will a business which sells on a cash basis.

Sometimes an overdraft facility will be needed to build up stock because of, or in anticipation of, an increase in sales volume. If stock does not sell as quickly as anticipated, then an overdraft might be needed in order for the business to meet its day-to-day needs.

Purpose

Is the facility which is being requested:

    (a)   A renewal of an existing limit?
    (b)   A new facility?
    (c)   An increased facility?

The need for an overdraft for working capital arises, for example:

    (a)   To finance increasing levels of sales.
    (b)   To finance the provision of longer credit terms to customers (probably in an attempt to increase sales).
    (c)   To finance larger stock holdings, e.g., a retailer wishing to offer more lines (leading hopefully to increased sales).

Amount

Is the amount being requested realistic?

A cash-flow forecast will be needed.

Has the cash-flow forecast been drawn up realistically?

27

(a)　Often the projected inflows are too optimistically timed resulting in excesses of the projected overdraft limit.

(b)　Have sales been realistically forecast?

If sales are increasing, will capital expenditure be needed? How will this be financed?

How does the amount requested compare with net worth?

Cash-flow forecast

The bank will check a forecast carefully and will question the assumptions on which the forecast is based:

(a)　Sales. This is the critical figure in the forecast. If the projected level of sales is not achieved, then the actual cash requirements will vary considerably from the forecast requirements. The bank will be wary of projections which are far more optimistic than past performance, and detailed explanations will be called for.

(b)　Credit terms. Does the forecast accurately reflect the credit terms received and given? For example, if in the past it has taken debtors around 50 days to pay, the forecast should not show that payment will be received in 30 days.

(c)　Relationship between debtors, creditors and bank balance. Longer credit being given than taken will normally result in the need for an overdraft (see Chapter 5). Is there flexibility in credit terms? If debtors are slow to pay, does the business have the option of delaying payment to suppliers, or will the result be an increase in the overdraft?

(d)　Overheads. What assumptions have been made in respect of overheads? Has each item been scrutinised or has an across-the-board percentage increase been applied? Are any one-off increases due, e.g., rent review?

(e)　Others. Where significant increases in sales are being forecast, has allowance been made in the cash forecast for increased labour, material and overhead costs, extra capital expenditure etc?

(f)　Monthly peaks. Forecasts for each month start with an opening balance and finish with a closing balance which reflects the net effect of inflows and outflows for that month. Forecasts do not show the peaks in borrowing which occur *during* the month. The bank will ask for such figures to be estimated.

Repayment

Calculate the cost of borrowing, i.e., interest on an average balance (cash-flow forecast can be used if provided).

Obviously no repayment programme of capital—in theory overdrafts disappear naturally as the need for them ceases to exist.

Remember that net profit shown in the accounts will have had interest on any existing overdraft already deducted. Therefore:

(a)   In respect of renewal of existing facility there will be no extra cost (assuming the same level of use).

(b)   In respect of a new facility there is no existing overdraft therefore there will be an extra cost.

(c)   In respect of an increased facility the amount of increase in the limit will create extra cost.

Can the business generate sufficient income to meet the extra cost of borrowing?

If the facility is to finance debtors, an age list will be needed to assess the likelihood of bad debts. Will factoring be more suitable?

The cash-flow forecast will indicate the ability of the business to generate sufficient cash to repay the overdraft.

Term

Maximum period 12 months (renewable).

Bank might ask for monthly figures for debtors, creditors and stock to monitor the position.

Security

Depends on type of business (see chapter 4).

Other factors

Usual considerations concerning length of connection etc.

Financing increasing sales can lead to overtrading—the bank will need to monitor situation closely.

8 | Overtrading

Overview

Overtrading is the term used when a business is expanding too quickly. It is difficult to define precisely, but it occurs when sales (and therefore costs) are increasing at such a rapid rate that cash cannot be generated quickly enough to support those sales. This results in creditors and lenders (mainly the bank) having to finance the turnover to an ever-increasing extent thus making the business vulnerable to creditor pressure.

A measure of overtrading may be inevitable and acceptable in, for example, new businesses. It is when it gets out of hand that problems arise. The bank and the creditors begin to lose confidence in the ability of the business to survive and consequently put pressure on the business to contract its activities.

Signs of overtrading

From the audited accounts:

(a)   Big increases in the level of sales in relation to the net worth of the business.

(b)   Big increases in the level of borrowed funds, in particular in short-term bank finance and in credit from suppliers.

From the bank account

(a)   Pressure on the overdraft limit, and excesses over the limit.

(b)   Less swing in the highest and lowest balances of the current account.

(c)   Increases in the average debit balance, showing heavier reliance on bank borrowing.

(d)   Hard-core borrowing developing, i.e., the current account is no longer swinging into credit. The hard-core is represented by the lowest debit balance.

Other signs:

(a) Issuing post-dated cheques—if this is done fairly frequently, it is a sign of cash-flow problems.

(b) Issuing cheques to suppliers for 'round' amounts. This indicates that only part of the full invoice is being paid 'on account'.

Too much should not be read into any one of these signs in isolation. It is where a number of them are present that the probability of over-trading can be assumed.

Audited accounts

It is impossible to be dogmatic about what is a reasonable relationship between sales and net worth. By the same token, this sign (or any other sign) in isolation is not evidence of overtrading. It is a combination of indicators which point towards that conclusion.

An increase in current liabilities to finance current assets will result in a deterioration in the current ratio (see Example 6.3, chapter 6). For example, if stock is increased by £10,000 as a result of an increase of £10,000 in the bank overdraft:

	Before	*After*
Current assets	£20,000	£30,000
Current liabilities	£10,000	£20,000
Current ratio	2:1	1.5:1

Paradoxically, if the current ratio was already less than 1:1, the ratio will improve:

	Before	*After*
Current assets	£10,000	£20,000
Current liabilities	£20,000	£30,000
Current ratio	0.5:1	0.67:1

Bank account

	19×1		*19×2*		*19×3*	
	£		£		£	
Limit	5,000		7,000		8,000	
High	5,600	Dr	7,300	Dr	8,200	Dr
Low	(1,200)	Cr	1,800	Dr	3,100	Dr
Average balance	4,400	Dr	6,100	Dr	7,300	Dr

Indicators

(a)   The overdraft limit is increasing—not in itself a bad sign because any expanding profitable business will need to increase its overdraft limit.

(b)   The swing into credit in the first year has now disappeared. Not necessarily bad—many sound, successful businesses may have periods when they do not get into credit.

(c)   Hard-core borrowing now developed and is increasing, i.e., £1,800 in the second year, and £3,100 in the third.

(d)   The average balance is high in relation to the limit. This shows that the overdraft is used extensively throughout the year.

(e)   Excesses seen over the limit. Would not necessarily be worrying if the average balance was less, as that would mean the excess was probably temporary. But linked to the high average debit balance, it shows that the account works near the limit throughout the year.

9 | Term Loans

Overview

Term loans are granted for the purchase of fixed assets such as premises, plant and machinery, vehicles, etc. The period of the loan will vary with the expected life of the asset, with the longer-term loans being used mainly for property purchases.

Purpose

What is being purchased?

(1) Existing premises at present being rented?
(2) Replacement premises involving a change of location?
(3) Additional premises?
(4) Plant and machinery?

The comments which follow will be numbered where relevant to correspond with the above categories.

Amount

In all cases, verification of the amount will be required.

In respect of premises, a professional valuation will be needed.

How does amount compare with net worth?

Will extra working capital be required especially in respect of (3) and (4)?

Repayment

In all cases, calculate the cost of borrowing and assess the business's ability to service the borrowing. Possibly pay only interest in the first year or two (capital holiday).

Note the following:

(a)   In respect of (1) there will be a rent saving.
(b)   In respect of (2) there will be the sale proceeds of the existing premises (if owned by the business).
(c)   In respect of (2) there will be disruption caused by the change of location. What effect will this have on productivity and profit?
(d)   In respect of (3) presumably the business is expanding. What increases in profit are expected and when? Extra plant and equipment will be needed. How is this to be financed? Extra labour will be needed thus increasing costs. How will this affect forecasts of future profits?
(e)   In respect of (4) is it replacement or additional? Will it increase efficiency and reduce production costs thus increasing profits?

Repayment calculations

In practice, banks will be able to obtain repayment figures from their computers or repayment tables. In the examination repayment tables will be given.

Term

Impossible to be dogmatic but as a rough guide:

(a)   Up to 25 years for premises.
(b)   Up to seven years for plant and machinery but no more than expected life span of equipment.

Security

Charge on any premises being bought.

Plant and machinery would be caught automatically by a debenture already held by bank but usually only under the floating charge. If the plant is particularly valuable, a specific fixed charge over it—a chattel mortgage—can be taken.

Other factors

Usual considerations, e.g., length of connection, etc.

Cross-sell asset insurance.

Practical considerations

With repayment spread over a medium or long term, the future prospects of the business constitute a vital part of the decision process.

(a) Will the business still be around in 10 years?
(b) How long have they been in business?
(c) What is their track record like?
(d) Is the management team capable and progressive in its thinking?
(e) Is there a good range of products with sound markets?

10 | Speculative Builders

Overview

A speculative builder is one who builds in the belief that there will be a ready market for the properties once they have been completed. The development could involve flats, offices etc., but these notes will concentrate on the building of houses.

In most cases the development will have to be phased. To fund the whole project before any properties are sold will usually involve too great a level of finance in relation to the size of the business. Phasing involves the building of an agreed number of houses for which the bank will provide finance, with further development being dependent on sales of some of the properties built in the first phase.

Purpose

The bank will want to see detailed planning permission.

The bank will require details of the project—how many houses, building costs, costs of roads and drainage etc., selling prices, cost of land, whether builder owns the land, whether a road bond is required, how long the project will take.

Amount

Has a detailed cash-flow forecast been prepared?

Up to twice net worth can be advanced provided the proposition is viable.

This will probably involve a phased development.

The size of the first phase will depend upon the amount the bank is prepared to lend, which in turn will depend upon the net worth of the builder.

Money will be lent in stages against architect's certificates, e.g., (a) foundations, (b) plate level (top of the walls), (c) roofing, (d) completion.

Does the amount being lent by the bank seem reasonable compared with one of the standard lending formulae?

What level of funds is being injected into the project by the builder?

Does the builder have a cash reserve for contingencies, e.g., delays caused by bad weather?

This subject is best explained by reference to an example, and the figures used are based on a past examination question.

Example 10.1

Project

To build six detached houses on land which cost £75,000 and which has been bought out of the builder's own resources, leaving the builder with cash resources of £25,000.

Costs

	£
Land	75,000
Construction	225,000
Roads etc.	10,000
Sundries	10,000
	320,000

Selling prices	£65,000 per house

The builder requests an overdraft of £250,000 to develop the site, which seems about right with the land having already been bought.

However the builder's net worth is only £70,000 and the bank will bear that in mind in deciding how much to lend. How much will be required to build two houses?

	£	
Construction	75,000	
Roads	10,000	(whole cost immediately)
Sundries	3,500	(one-third)
	88,500	

Notes

(a)　This amount exceeds net worth but since there is an identifiable source of funds to repay the advance, the position is not too serious.

(b)　The cost of roads etc. cannot be phased.

(c)　The builder has a reserve of cash to meet contingencies.

(d)　How does the advance compare with the standard lending formulae for speculative building? (See example 10.3.)

(e)　A lending of (say) £90,000 would seem reasonable but it will be virtually impossible to monitor the repayment programme unless the lending is made on a separate loan account.

Repayment

This will come from sale proceeds of the houses.

The bank will arrange with the builder to take a proportion of the proceeds of each sale, sufficient to repay the advance and interest, by the time the development of the site is (say) two-thirds completed.

Provided that the bank is not too greedy in the amount taken from each sale, no further funds will need to be provided for further phases—the amount advanced for the first phase will be reduced by the agreed portion of proceeds from each sale.

The bank will need to be satisfied that the houses will sell at the asking price—an estate agent's opinion will be obtained.

The houses will not sell unless mortgages are available—it is important that the builder is registered with the National House Builders Council, otherwise it might be difficult for would-be purchasers to obtain a mortgage.

Example 10.2

The bank has advanced £90,000 for the first phase, involving two houses. The objectives are:

(a)　Not to have to lend again for later phases.

(b)　To obtain repayment of £90,000 plus interest of (say) £10,000 from the sale proceeds of the first four houses, i.e., when the development is two-thirds completed.

Therefore the bank needs to recover (say) £100,000 from the sale proceeds of four houses—selling price £65,000. The bank will agree with the builder to take £25,000 from each sale, leaving the builder with £40,000 for further building work.

The bank might agree a slighly more flexible repayment programme by taking only £15,000 from the first sale, £25,000 from *each* of the next two, and £35,000 from the fourth. This will help the builder's cash-flow in the early part of the development.

Should there be any delays in construction or sale, or should interest rates rise resulting in higher finance costs, the bank might not be fully repaid by the sale of the fourth house. However, there are still two properties to be sold, and there should be no problem in any small excess being cleared by the sale of the fifth house.

Term

This depends on the building programme and the saleability of the houses.

It will be prudent to add a further six months to the builder's expectations of how long the project will take.

Security

A charge over the building land with each plot being released from the charge when sale proceeds are received.

The deeds (or land certificate or charge certificate) will be held by a solicitor against an undertaking in relation to the sale proceeds.

Status enquiry on solicitor, if not known.

Other factors

Is the size of this project within the builder's capabilities and past experience?

Has he got access to sufficient labour and equipment?

Will work have to be subcontracted? Can the necessary control be exercised?

Is a road bond required by the local authority? If so, what effect will this have on the amount the bank is prepared to lend? How real a liability is it likely to be? This will depend on the track record of the builder—if he is experienced then the potential liability for the bank will be minimal.

Example 10.3

The textbook formula for speculative builders is: half cost of land, two-thirds development costs for the first phase. Applying this to the example:

	£
$\frac{1}{2}$ cost of land	37,500
$\frac{2}{3}$ development costs	50,000
	87,500

This is in line with the proposed lending of £90,000.

A more popular guideline with bankers is to assess the builder's contribution, which will be expected to be at least:

$\frac{1}{3}$ cost of land (or current valuation, if lower)
$\frac{1}{3}$ of roads, drainage etc.
$\frac{1}{2}$ development costs for first phase

In our example, the builder was contributing £100,000 (land purchase plus cash reserve of £25,000). Applying the guideline, his minimum contribution should be:

	£
$\frac{1}{3}$ cost of land	25,000
$\frac{1}{3}$ roads, drainage	3,500
$\frac{1}{2}$ development costs	37,500
	66,000

Therefore, the builder is making a significant contribution to the project.

It should be remembered that a phased development is only necessary where the amount requested is too great in relation to net worth. Similarly, if a builder has substantial funds due to be received from other developments or other sources, a phased development might not be necessary. The advance to the builder in that case, might be more in the nature of a bridging advance pending receipt of the funds.

Each situation has to be looked at carefully and treated on its merits.

11 | Contract Builders

Overview

Contract builders are different to speculative builders in that repayment of any advance does *not* come from the sale of the houses.

They are contracted to build by (for example) a local authority and they receive payment from the authority on a regular basis (usually monthly).

Payment is made by the authority against a surveyor's or architect's certificate of work done and the contract will usually allow the authority to retain part of the proceeds due to the contractor until the contract is complete.

Security can sometimes be a problem because the contractor will not own the land being developed.

Purpose

The bank will want to see the contract.

Is the customer experienced in this type of work?

The contract

Unless completely satisfied with the experience and past record of the customer, the bank will want to inspect the contract in respect of the following:

   (a)   Is the contract price fixed or variable? The builder will be vulnerable to increases in material and labour costs if the contract price is fixed.

   (b)   Penalty clauses for late completion of work, which will affect the builder's cashflow and profit. The contract might have flexibility built into it to allow for bad weather etc.

   (c)   The payment terms, i.e., the frequency with which the work will be inspected (usually monthly) and how long after that before payment is received.

(d)   Retentions. These are moneys retained by the employer until the contract is complete. Up to 10% is deducted and retained by the employer from each payment made to the contractor, with an overall maximum figure.

(e)   Period after completion of contract before retention moneys are released. This is usually around six months during which period defects in the work could become apparent which the contractor has to rectify.

Amount

A cash-flow forecast will be needed showing maximum level of overdraft required.

The bank will inspect the forecast with the following points in mind:

(a)   Has allowance been made for the fact that probably no money will be received until the end of the second month? The surveyor will inspect work at the end of the first month but payment might not be received for a further month.

(b)   Has allowance been made for late inspection by the surveyor?

(c)   Has the effect of retentions been allowed for?

(d)   Is there any margin to allow for delays in work caused by bad weather?

(e)   Is sufficient plant and labour allowed for?

Repayment

The bank will want to see the contractor's costings of work to be done in order to assess the profitability of the contract.

If the contract is sufficiently profitable, it represents an identifiable source of repayment, i.e., the overdraft will be repaid by the contract moneys.

In such circumstances, the bank might be prepared to lend in excess of net worth.

The financial standing of the employer is vital, i.e., local authority or whoever it is. Bank might make status enquiry.

Term

This depends on the size of the contract and the schedule of work.

The bank will be able to estimate the term approximately from the cash-flow forecast.

Security

The bank will often have to rely on the customer's own assets (if any) because usually the land being developed will not be available as security.

Other factors

The track record of the customer with similar types of contract will be important.

Who is responsible for insurance—employer or contractor?

The customer must be able to demonstrate the necessary technical and managerial skills.

The ability to cost the job properly will be crucial.

Security problem

There might be a building contract under which the contractor agrees to build on land owned by the employer, for an agreed sum of money. The bank might take charge over the future debt which the contract represents. But the debt would not be good security if the contract is not completed to the satisfaction of the employer for any reason.

12 | Buying a Business

Overview

This type of proposition is seen frequently both in practice and in examination papers. One of the major obstacles is the customer's over-optimism about what can be achieved in the business, and the banker has to take a level-headed, objective view of any projections which are produced. Adequate security can often be a problem if the purchase does not include the freehold of the premises.

Purpose

Does the customer have the necessry skill, aptitude and experience to run the business?

Apart from any technical skills which might be necessary, does the customer have any business acumen?

Why is the previous owner selling? Retirement, ill-health, poor living from the business?

Is living accommodation included?

Business experience

The question of previous experience has to be treated flexibly. Very often, proposals are received from customers who have left their employment to set up in business and cannot, therefore, demonstrate previous involvement.

Only if the business requires specialist or technical skills should this aspect be of paramount importance. There are many businesses which can be run adequately with common sense. A measure of financial awareness is obviously needed but a good accountant will provide assistance generally, and in particular with any forecasts which the bank might require.

Provided the bank has adequate security, with a good margin, and the customer is aware of the risks involved, the lack of previous experience should not be a stumbling-block.

Amount

How is the purchase price of the business made up? Is stock included?

Are the assets of the business over-valued?

How has goodwill been calculated? Two to three times net profit would be reasonable (impossible to be dogmatic).

Is stock good and saleable?

Will fixtures and fittings need to be replaced in near future?

Have short leases been adequately depreciated?

Will working capital be required?

The customer must make a reasonable contribution to the cost of the business. Source of customer's funds?

Repayment

Has the customer obtained figures for sales, profits etc?

Is the business viable? Location is important.

Are sufficient profits being generated to service bank borrowing and provide the customer with an adequate standard of living?

Can a profit forecast be drawn up?

(a) The customer will probably over-estimate the level of sales to be achieved. The customer's experience or lack of it will affect what can be achieved.

(b) The bank will be sceptical of forecasts of sales and profit margins which are better than the previous owner achieved. Customer will have to justify.

(c) Did the previous owner have the benefit of better terms with suppliers than the customer can obtain?

(d) With short leases, when is the next rent review due? What is the increase likely to be?

(e) What level of drawings will the customer require?

(f) Has a detailed breakdown of overheads been undertaken?

Term

Cost of business should be granted on a term loan.

Period will depend on amount and ability to repay.

Anything up to (say) 10 years would be reasonable.

That part of the purchase price relating to stock should be granted on overdraft.

Security

Charge can be taken over lease although it is not ideal security (see under 'Short leases' below). However, a charge will ensure the bank gets repaid on a voluntary sale.

Purchase price might include freehold of shop—charge can be taken.

Has the customer any personal security to offer?

Life insurance on proprietor always necessary.

Short leases

These are usually poor security because:

 (a)   They are difficult to value.
 (b)   They depreciate in value.
 (c)   The lease will be forfeited if rent is not paid.
 (d)   They often contain clauses which provide for the forfeiture of the lease in the event of the bankruptcy or liquidation of the lessee. Therefore, at a time when the bank will want to rely on the lease as security, it will be unavailable.

Other factors

Usual considerations concerning character, past record etc.

Cross-sell insurance (e.g., stock, buildings if relevant), pensions.

Franchising

This is a popular way to start out in business. The purchaser in effect buys a licence to use the name of a nationally recognised organization. The purchaser enjoys the benefits which the organisation brings (e.g., guidance on stocking, pricing, administration, finance) and in return pays a percentage of takings to the franchisor. The risks of failure are therefore reduced, although not eliminated altogether as franchisors can fail also.

All banks have specially tailored franchise loan schemes to assist with establishment costs, payment for the licence and working capital. The customer's contribution should be at least one-third of total cost and the term should not exceed the period for which the licence has been granted.

13 | Farmers

Overview

Lending to farmers is feared by most examination candidates but it contains less specialist features than speculative building, for example.

The approach will be strongly influenced by the purpose of the advance as some will generate extra revenue whilst others will not.

Values of farm land can fluctuate considerably over periods of time and according to geographical area. Sales of land to tenant farmers can often be at a price which contains a substantial hidden reserve.

Purpose

Farmers might need to borrow typically for the following reasons:

(a)   Working capital, e.g., pending harvest proceeds.
(b)   To build up stock of animals—this will generate extra income eventually.
(c)   Purchase of farm land—this will generate extra income only if it is *additional* land. The purchase of existing rented land will not generate income.

Amount

The bank will want to see some evidence of amount, e.g., cash-flow forecast, valuation of land (if relevant).

How does the amount compare with the net worth of the farmer?

If land is being bought, what is the price per acre? Is this reasonable for the land quality and the area?

There could be a hidden reserve, especially if existing rented land is being bought—this will boost net worth.

If additional land is being bought, consider whether extra working capital will be required.

Repayment

Calculate the cost of borrowing and assess the farmer's ability to service borrowing.

A projected budget is required. The income shown will be affected by the purpose of the lending.

The purchase of existing rented land will provide a rent saving which will increase funds available for repayment.

Ability to repay

A number of measures can be used to assess a farmer's ability to service financial obligations. An individual budget on expected yields and levels of expenditure is preferred but the banker can apply rough tests in the form of rental equivalent on its own and as a percentage of gross output.

In its broadest form, rental equivalent is the total of all financial charges (including rent and rates so that tenant and owner-occupier farmers are treated the same) divided by the number of acres. Anything over £60 per acre is regarded as being a high cost to service, although dairy farming can normally carry up to around £90 per acre.

A more accurate measure is rental equivalent as a percentage of gross output (sales in its broadest form). Anything over 15% would be seen as being a high cost to service.

Term

Up to 25 years for land purchase.

Security

Charge on any land purchased.

Security value will be boosted by any hidden reserve.

Bank might take (or have) an agricultural charge (not possible if farm is a limited company but could then take debenture).

Agricultural charge

An agricultural charge is a little like a debenture in nature in that it charges the whole of the farm assets to the bank, with one or two notable exceptions.

An agricultural charge does not include debtors nor the farm land itself which is charged in the normal manner, by way of legal mortgage.

Other factors

Usual considerations, concerning length of connection etc.

Capability of farmer is important—are yields above average?

Farm visit can reveal important facts, e.g., condition of buildings, equipment, animals.

Has the farmer provided a confidential statement of assets and liabilities—usually a more realistic assessment than audited accounts?

14 | Import Finance

Overview

Goods being imported may be either finished goods or raw materials.

The bank might be asked:

(a) To issue an irrevocable letter of credit in respect of the transaction. This guarantees payment to the overseas seller provided he complies strictly with the terms of the credit.

(b) To lend against the value of the goods in the form of a produce advance.

Purpose

The importer asks the bank to open a letter of credit (usually irrevocable) in favour of the overseas supplier.

Are goods to be on-sold to a known buyer or to be stored in a warehouse pending sale or processing?

Will the importer be invoiced in sterling or foreign currency?

The bank will want any exchange risk to be covered in the forward market.

Amount

Is the customer good for the amount of the credit?

Will the customer have sufficient funds to meet the credit when due?

How does the liability compare with net worth when added to the customer's other facilities?

The bank might be generous because of the short-term self-liquidating nature of the advance.

51

Line of credit

For established importers, the bank will provide a line of credit, i.e., a limit marked for documentary credits. Then bank will then continue to open credits provided the amount of all credits outstanding does not exceed the limit.

The issue of an irrevocable credit is a real liablity for the bank as payment must be made to the exporter if he has complied with the credit terms, irrespective of whether the bank can debit the customer's account.

The amount advanced on a produce advance is not likely to be more than 80% of the value of the goods. The other 20% has to be provided by the customer in cash or (for established importers) can be debited to the current account within an agreed overdraft facility.

Repayment

This will come from the sale proceeds of the goods.

Is there a definite buyer?

Is the buyer good for the amount?

Is a status report required?

Is there a ready market for the goods if the bank is left with them due to the customer being unable to meet the obligation?

Term

Short-term, self-liquidating advance when goods are pre-sold.

In respect of warehoused goods, the term will depend on the state of the market for those goods.

Security

It is vital that the bank has possession of the shipping documents so that control can be exercised over the goods.

The bank will release the documents to the importer so that delivery of the goods from the ship can be taken. The importer gives the bank a trust letter, in which he undertakes to let the bank have the sale proceeds (if pre-sold) or to warehouse the goods in the bank's name (pending sale).

The bank takes a letter of pledge over warehoused goods, which have to be stored in the name of the bank. This again gives the bank control of the goods.

The bank will usually have around 20% security cover (having advanced 80% of the invoice value of the goods).

Other factors

Is the overseas seller reliable? Will the customer receive the correct goods in the right quantity, quality etc. Bank might insist on a certificate of inspection under the terms of the credit.

Is the customer reliable? Can the bank rely on the customer's trust letter?

Goods must be insured at all times. When warehoused, notice of the bank's interest must be endorsed on the policy.

Has the customer complied with import licence requirements?

The bank will inspect goods in warehouse from time to time.

15 | Export Finance

Overview

Export finance usually takes the form of either advances against bills being collected, or bills discounted.

In both cases, the financial strength of the drawee is vital as this is the source of repayment, although both facilities will usually be granted with recourse to the exporter.

Purpose

Bill finance is a short-term facility which can be used as an alternative to overdraft.

Have the bills been properly drawn (and accepted where applicable)?

Who is the acceptor? The overseas buyer or a bank?

Amount

How does the requested facility compare with net worth when added to the exporter's other borrowing?

The bank might be prepared to lend in excess of net worth because of the short-term nature of the lending but much will depend on the financial standing of the drawee and/or whether the exporter has ECGD cover.

The bank will advance a proportion of each bill being collected according to the quality of the drawee.

Bills discounted will be 100% finance less interest charges.

Line of credit

The bank usually grants a line of credit, i.e., agrees a limit up to which it will provide finance. The limit might be generous in relation to net worth because the facility is short-term with an identifiable source of repayment.

The bank might impose some of the following conditions:

(a)   The proportion to be advanced against each bill (applicable only to bills being collected).

(b)   Bills to be drawn at not more than 180 days.

(c)   Bills payable in the UK.

(d)   Bills to be drawn in sterling (if drawn in currency the exchange risk must be covered forward).

(e)   Exporter must have ECGD insurance cover.

(f)   No individual bill to be drawn for more than (say) 20% of the facility.

(g)   Limits on exposure to certain countries.

Repayment

This comes from the proceeds of the bill at maturity.

The bank will carry out status reports on buyers.

The bank will have recourse to the exporter, should the overseas buyer default. Is the exporter good to meet dishonoured bills plus incidental costs?

Does the exporter have the benefit of ECGD cover to protect against default by buyer?

ECGD cover

Banks will prefer exporters to have an ECGD comprehensive short-term policy, which provides cover of 90% of net invoice value. However, ECGD cover is no guarantee of payment because ECGD will not pay out if the exporter has failed to fulfil any of the conditions set out in the policy.

It is vital therefore that the customer is not only technically capable of carrying out the contract with the overseas buyer, but can meet also the terms of the ECGD policy.

Term

Maximum maturity date of bills is 180 days.

Security

The bank might take a letter of hypothecation over bills being collected.

A debenture given to another lender would have priority over the letter of hypothecation.

In such circumstances, bank would have to discount bills rather than advance against collections.

The bank could also take an assignment of any ECGD policy.

Other factors

The track record of the exporter is vitally important because of the problems which can arise when exporting, e.g., default of buyer, goods left on quayside of an overseas port etc.

ECGD policies lay down strict conditions with which the exporter must comply otherwise a claim will be refused.

How experienced is the exporter in handling ECGD policy obligations?

Have claims been refused in the past?

Other facilities for exporters

Medium-term loans of up to 10 years can be made in respect of the export of capital goods. Finance can be made available to either the supplier or the buyer. ECGD will guarantee up to 85% of the contract price.

Forfaiting. The bank buys at a discount a series of bills from the exporter with maturities spread over a period of up to five years, usually in respect of the supply of capital goods. The facility is provided without recourse to the exporter, and therefore it is vital that the bills have been avalised (guaranteed) by the buyer's bank.

Countertrade. The exporter might have to accept, in part or total settlement, goods of the country to which he is exporting, rather than cash. The bank might be able to assist in finding a buyer for the goods.

16 | New Ventures

Overview

This topic can cover a wide area. It can be a customer with a new product or service for which finance is required to launch the business. It can be a customer established in one area of business wanting to diversify into something new. It could simply be a customer wanting to buy a unit in a newly developed shopping block.

In all cases, the major point is that there is no proven track record to which the lending banker can refer. The customer will have to provide detailed projections of potential sales, profitability and cash requirements, and the need for adequate security is obvious.

Purpose

New product or service:

(a)   How certain is the customer that there is a need or market for the product or service?

(b)   Has any research been undertaken professionally? The bank will wish to see the results.

(c)   Has the customer undertaken any personal research?

Diversification:

(a)   Why has the customer chosen that particular area of activity?

(b)   Is it linked in any way to existing activities? Will there be spin-offs?

(c)   Does the customer have specialist skills and experience in the chosen area?

(d)   Why does the customer believe that he or she will be successful?

New unit:

(a)   What type of business will the customer be engaged in?
(b)   Is there a need or market?
(c)   Is the location right?
(d)   Is there competition nearby? Is it strong and well established?

Amount

The customer will be expected to make a significant contribution as this is a high-risk area of lending. The bank will not want to be taking a bigger risk than the customer.

The customer will need to provide a detailed cash flow forecast. The bank will take a more pessimistic view than the customer has done.

The bank will query the cash flow:

    (a)   What credit terms have been agreed with suppliers?

    (b)   Will credit terms be offered to customers? How much credit? Is this about right for this line of business? Will this generate the level of sales projected?

    (c)   What stocking levels are regarded as being appropriate?

    (d)   Have overheads been realistically assessed?

The bank will ensure that all these considerations have been catered for in the cash-flow forecast.

Repayment

The customer will need to provide a detailed budget forecast of sales and profits.

The bank will pay special attention to the following points:

    (a)   What level of sales is being projected? Is this achievable? On what has the customer based the projection?

    (b)   What level of profits is being projected? Are the margins realistic?

    (c)   Have any items of expenditure been overlooked or under-stated?

    (d)   Will any capital expenditure be required?

    (e)   How much has been allocated for drawings?

    (f)   Has interest been included?

    (g)   Has a break-even analysis been undertaken?

Projections

Whenever projections are produced in any lending proposition, the banker has to query the assumptions on which the projections are based. This is particularly important where new ventures are concerned because, obviously, there is no track record to act as a guide.

The banker needs to carry out some sort of sensitivity analysis to see what the effect would be on profit and cash projections if actual figures varied from the budgets, e.g., if sales were 20% less, if customers took an extra 30 days to pay, and so on.

Provided the sensitivity analysis is done realistically, the banker will ascertain the customer's worst position and will be able to form a judgment as to the acceptability of that position.

There might not be sufficient time in the examination to carry out a sensitivity analysis, but reference should at least be made to the fact that projections are probably optimistic.

Term

This will depend on the circumstances.

Capital holidays could be arranged in the early stages of any term loan.

Security

This is high-risk lending, therefore the bank will need to be well secured.

The bank will want to be able to recover the lending quickly and conveniently should things go wrong.

Other factors

All banks have tailored schemes for new ventures.

Interest rates can be either fixed or variable.

For larger projects, the bank might provide venture capital—perhaps a combination of loan and equity—taking a minority stake in the business.

The usual considerations concerning character etc. will apply.

What if things go wrong?

The failure rate of new ventures is high, and the bank needs to consider what its position will be if things do go wrong. Obviously there will be no on-going business which can be sold, and the bank will therefore be left looking to its security for repayment.

It is important both for the bank and the customer in such a situation that the lending can be recovered quickly and conveniently. Liquid personal assets such as stocks and shares or life policies would be ideal. A second charge over the matrimonial home would take time and a great deal of inconvenience to realise. Business assets would probably be depleted and have a realisation value well below book value.

The customer's attitude to the realising of security is very important, especially personal assets, and in particular the house. Will the customer be cooperative in the circumstances or will the banker be faced with obstacles? Character and integrity are vital features but favourable past impressions might count for little when the customer's home is being sold. Ideally, when taking the family home as security, there should be sufficient equity left after the sale to rehouse the customer in a more modest property.

17 | Buying a Small Hotel or Guest-House

Overview

This type of business is seen mainly in tourist areas and therefore many bankers will be unfamiliar with the features of it. There are no past examination questions on this subject, but that does mean that it will not be examined in the future.

Purpose

This is a specialised type of business which requires attention 24 hours a day. Is the borrower the right type of person for this?

The business requires someone with drive, commitment, good health, friendly attitude to guests, helpful, nothing too much trouble to do for guests.

Does the borrower have any previous experience in this type of business? If not, then the risks of failure are greater, and the bank will have to ensure it is well secured.

Ideally, the borrower should be responsible for day-to-day management, ensuring active involvement.

Will members of the family be involved? Do they also possess the necessary personal attributes? They should be involved in the key areas which deal directly with guests, e.g., reception, bar etc.

Is the hotel in good repair and good decorative order? If not, will finance be required to bring it up to the required standard? Any work will have to be done out of season to ensure no disruption to guests.

Amount

How is the purchase price made up? What is the breakdown for premises, fixtures and fittings, furnishings, stock, goodwill?

The borrower should have an independent valuation done.

61

How much is the borrower contributing? It is impossible to be dogmatic about an acceptable level of contribution. For example, a low contribution to buy a successful business where the borrower is highly experienced, is a better proposition than a high contribution for a stagnant business where the borrower is inexperienced and therefore unlikely to be able to improve matters.

Have legal costs been allowed for?

Will any working capital be required?

Repayment

Is a breakdown available of income from the different activities, i.e., room letting, bar etc.

Presumably, repayment will come from cash flow.

Cash flow will be seasonal.

Repayment might be matched to cash flow, i.e., the borrower pays interest only 'out of season'.

What is the pattern of the business? Does it rely mainly on 'one-off' bookings, or is there significant repeat business? Obviously, the latter reduces the risk in respect of repayment.

With this size of hotel there is no likelihood of conference business, but it could be used for regular meetings by local groups. This could provide 'out of season' business.

Do they advertise in the local brochure? Do they do bargain breaks etc?

The bank should review advance bookings in (say) March/April each year as a guide to expected levels of cash flow during the summer.

Repayment prospects can be improved if the borrower takes 'out of season' employment.

Term

Anything up to 20 years would be acceptable for this type of proposition.

Security

The bank will require a legal charge over the premises.

It would be prudent to discount heavily the valuation of premises for security purposes, because should the business fail, the premises may have only 'bricks and mortar' value as there will be no ongoing business to sell. A prudent assessment would be 40% of valuation.

Life cover on the borrower is essential.

Buildings and contents insurance is essential.

Other factors

The hotel must have a current fire certificate to show that it complies with fire regulations. It could add greatly to the cost if the hotel does not meet the regulations at present.

A visit should be made to the hotel to see it as a guest would see it. The success of the business will depend on factors such as: bright pleasant surroundings, cleanliness, good decorative order, amenities, car parking, attitude of staff etc.

The asset structure of the business should be predominantly fixed assets. Current assets for this type of business are comparatively low, i.e., there should be few debtors, food stock should be low etc.

Goodwill is likely to be a large, significant asset.

PART B   BANKING SERVICES

1 | Variable-rate Facilities

Synopsis of service

(a) Overdraft—fluctuating renewable facility whereby a limit is agreed, for periodic review, at the outset with interest charged only when the borrowing is drawn. Usually no allowance given for credit balance for corporate customers, although banks are now introducing schemes for rewarding personal customer credit balances.

(b) Loan—may be short, medium or long term—as long as 25 years in some cases. Limit is agreed at the outset and funds drawn as required. Agreement may include options to revolve and roll over (see part B, chapter 4).

Drawings for both overdrafts and loans may be in sterling or currency, or a combination.

Interest may be charged as:

(a) A percentage over the lender's published base rate—which will vary from time to time in line with market trends. This method is used for personal and smaller business borrowings.

(b) A flat mortgage rate for personal house loans.

(c) A percentage over LIBOR (London interbank offered rate), generally finer than base rate, but more variable and suitable for only a limited market (see part B, chapter 4).

All personal borrowings up to £15,000 are subject to the Consumer Credit Act 1974.

Suitable cases

Overdraft

Day-to-day personal expenditure, or short-term trading needs across all types of business (including farming).

It may be efficient cash management to invest sizeable credit balances, and meet short-term cash-flow shortages from an overdraft facility.

Loans

Usually for customers wishing to fund a capital item over the natural life of the item. For those who prefer not to fix the interest rate at the outset often anticipating a fall in base rate or LIBOR, or intending to repay prior to maturity.

Personal customers who wish to spread the cost of a specific expenditure without necessarily fixing the interest rate may use variable-rate loans.

Marketing benefits

Overdraft

Flexibility enabling opportunities to be taken as they arise, discounts obtained for prompt payment and avoidance of penalties for late payment of creditors.

Availability of finance provides peace of mind.

Efficient cash management capabilities allowing investment of credit balances with cash-flow hiccups accommodated from overdraft.

Loan

Firm commitment from the lender for a specific period.

Enables repayments to be spread over a suitable term so as not to affect cash flow adversely—the term of the loan matches the purpose.

Segregates the expenditure for a specific purpose from normal cash flow.

Interest rates are market linked (LIBOR being more volatile than base rate) resulting in savings when rates fall, but conversely increased costs on rising trends.

Costs

Interest charges

Range from 1% above base rate for 'blue chip' borrowers, to 12% above base rate for unauthorised borrowing. Risk, availability of security and terms are the major factors in setting a rate—usually 3% or 4% over base rate for an agreed facility.

For larger corporate borrowers with loans linked to LIBOR, margins below 1% are frequently negotiated.

Arrangement fee

Negotiable—usually up to 1% to recognise the work involved in putting a facility together.

Commitment or non-utilisation fee

Negotiable—usually up to $\frac{1}{2}$% to recognise the opportunity costs of putting aside sufficiet funds to cover the capital adequacy costs in respect of the commitment.

The longer the period of commitment, the higher the commitment fee.

2 | Fixed-rate Facilities

Synopsis of service

Personal

Personal loan—a generally unsecured committed facility with interest rates agreed at a published flat rate in advance. Repayments, inclusive of interest, are spread over the term of the loan usually up to five years. Life assurance and health and redundancy insurance during the currency of the loan are available as optional additions.

Home improvement loans—similar arrangement to personal loans, but term can be up to 10 years.

All personal borrowings up to £15,000 are subject to the Consumer Credit Act 1974.

Corporate

Business development loans—committed loans on a fixed-interest basis. May be secured or unsecured, but a finer rate attaches to secured facilities. Term can be as long as 25 years, but usually up to 10 years with finer rates for the shorter term. Repayments inclusive of interest are made on a monthly basis.

Life assurance is available as an optional extra, and is usually recommended. Capital repayment holidays of usually up to two years are available on most facilities of this nature.

Fixed-rate loans—for larger corporates these can be made available on a medium-term loan, but are more usually seen as short-term money-market loans.

All fixed-rate loans will carry a penalty for early repayment.

Suitable cases

Personal

Typically car purchase, season-ticket loans, holiday loans etc., or improvements to property, where the borrower prefers not to extend a mortgage.

Corporate

Either individuals or corporates involved in business, professions or industry, who have a capital or start-up need, and seek fixed monthly repayments inclusive of interest.

Marketing benefits

Personal customers

Usually unsecured.

Agreed quickly—usually credit scored.

Fixed interest rate from the outset with fixed monthly reductions enabling ease of cash-flow management.

Flexible term to suit purpose.

Optional death or redundancy insurance cover.

Sometimes incorporate hardship clause affording sympathetic arrangements in the event of difficulties.

Corporate customers

Flexibility of purpose.

Certainty of monthly repayment levels to aid budgeting and planning.

Enables purchase of assets against limited cash resources.

Firm commitment.

Capital holiday options.

Options for early repayment subject to a specified penalty.

Costs

Setting-up fee of up to 1%.

Interest rate—fixed at the outset and shown as both a flat and annualised rate.

Interest rates for secured facilities are calculated on a finer basis than unsecured.

3 | Venture Capital Finance

Synopsis of service

Usually takes the form of a subordinated loan, ranking behind creditor claims, but in front of proprietor's interests.

An equity option giving the investor an option to purchase a minority percentage of the company's share capital, either in the form of preference or ordinary shares, is usually attached.

Often referred to as 'mezzanine' finance, facilities can be provided for durations of up to 10 years, through the clearing banks' venture capital subsidiaries and from merchant banks.

Capital and interest repayment holidays can be negotiated usually for up to two years; interest is often received by way of dividend.

Such facilities are generally unsecured, although the unsupported guarantees of the directors are usually sought.

Various specialist organisations exist for the provision of venture capital; these often complement existing and more traditional bank lines.

Suitable cases

Corporate customers often with new ventures and sound management. Potential has been identified but resources have been exhausted usually on research and prototype investment. Finance is required either for working capital, or capital expenditure. However, venture capital is equally relevant for existing operations looking to expand.

Evidence of ability with (for existing companies) track record is sought, and key man insurance is often appropriate.

Marketing benefits

Provision of needed finance, frequently not available from more traditional sources of finance.

Investment can be treated as quasi capital and as such improves the company's debt gearing, rather than deteriorating it.

The repayment holidays can be of particular benefit in the early formative years.

Subject to there being no breaches of covenants, the line is committed for an agreed term.

Customer retains control of the company, i.e., retains a majority shareholding but the albeit minority shareholding will provide direct access to experienced financial management—frequently the lender seems to place a representative on the borrower's board.

Flexibility of venture capital packages means that repayment schemes can be tailored to meet the precise needs of the customer.

Costs

Loan facilities will be extended at similar rates to standard borrowing prices, and will normally involve a commitment and/or arrangement fee of up to 1%.

For arrangements in the form of equity participations, dividend payments will replace the interest charges, and income to the bank will depend upon performance.

4 | Corporate Finance

Synopsis of service

Major corporates are able to supplement the traditional sources of finance to obtain wholesale funds in the following ways:

(a) Acceptance credits whereby the company draws up bills of exchange drawn on itself (up to 180 days maturity) which an eligible bank accepts. The bill is then discounted, either by the bank or in the discount market with the company realising the value of the bill, less the cost of discount and the acceptance commission.

(b) Commercial paper, similar to acceptance credits, but slightly more risky due to the fact that only the issuing company is liable, whereas an investor in a bill drawn under an acceptance credit can look to the accepting bank as well as the drawer.

(c) Market lines whereby the borrower has, through its bank dealers, direct access to the money market and can take money, plus a negotiated margin (usually also plus mandatory liquid assets (MLAs) for UK sterling) at market rates. This is sometimes documented as a line 'at the bank's option' whereby there is no compulsion to lend if the bank is short of funds.

(d) Multi-option facilities (MOFs) are combination facilities, which enable the borrower to choose from a selection of lending vehicles. The list is documented at the outset and the borrower has complete freedom of choice thereafter.

Suitable cases

Major corporates with substantial borrowing needs which are administered by an internal treasury department. The borrowings will often be reviewed on a daily basis, and the most efficient mix of vehicles used—e.g., acceptance credits and commercial paper for needs up to, say, three months, with market lines used to balance the overnight shortfall.

Marketing benefits

Ability to access the market at very fine rates—commercial paper usually at sub-LIBOR for good credits—determined by the rating set by the credit agencies.

Flexibility of choosing specific borrowing facility to meet precise need—lines will frequently offer a multi-currency option.

Costs

Borrowing costs will be a mix of interest rates, commitment fees, and administration costs—particularly in the case of a bank acting as issuing and paying agent under a commercial paper programme. Such fees will be negotiable, whereas the interest rate will be a reflection of (a) the quality of the borrower, and (b) the liquidity of the market.

Rates will be quoted as a margin related to LIBOR. Insofar as investors in commercial paper are liquid companies who would otherwise invest (often with banks) they are prepared to lend at rates between the deposit and lending rates and hence frequently will lend at margins *below* LIBOR.

The Bank of England rules relating to capital adequacy require banks to maintain set liquidity margins against lending and the costs of doing so will be added to the interest margin.

5 | Leasing

Synopsis of service

Arrangement whereby the lessor purchases an asset, obtaining any available tax benefits, then 'rents' the item to the lessee, passing on some benefit by way of reduced 'rental'.

With an *operating lease* the lessor is responsible for maintenance and servicing, and the term of the lease is not necessarily for the full economic life of the asset—i.e., there is a secondary period when the item may be leased to another lessee for a good rental. A typical example of an operating lease would be a 'contract hire' arrangement for a car fleet.

With a *finance lease*, whilst the lessor has ownership of the item, the lessee takes delivery of it, and is responsible for its upkeep, servicing etc. The term of the lease is for a 'primary period' which recognises the anticipated useful life of the asset, after which time it may be sold, with a percentage of the proceeds being retained by the lessee. Alternatively it may be continued to be leased at a 'peppercorn rent' (a notional figure) for a secondary term.

Lease purchase is effectively hire-purchase—see part B, chapter 6.

Suitable cases

Companies in need of a capital item, yet with insufficient resources for outright purchase and an insufficient profit performance to enjoy full tax writing-down allowances (following the Finance Act 1984).

Companies preferring to keep the asset off balance sheet, hence improving the return-on-assets performance and gearing calculation. This is only possible through the use of operating leases. Finance leases are regarded as 'on' balance sheet.

Where items of a specialist nature are involved—those susceptible to technological change or regular maintenance (e.g., computers, cars)—and the customer prefers to 'buy' a package including all maintenance costs.

Marketing benefits

Provision of tax benefits by available writing-down allowances which may otherwise have been lost through an inadequate level of profitability.

Rental payments are paid out of the profit and loss account hence reducing the ultimate taxable profit.

Usually no initial capital expenditure is required.

Avoids maintaining an asset register and the need to calculate depreciation.

Assists budgeting and cash-flow forecasting as costs are fixed and maintenance charges covered.

In finance leases, often the sale proceeds will provide a generous refund.

Whilst operating leases are 'off balance sheet', finance leases are now considered as 'on balance sheet' items and must be included in performance measures. None the less the other benefits remain apposite.

Costs

Costs are flexible having regard to the standing of the customer, period of lease, prevailing interest rate and the type of asset, but the lessor will structure the rental arrangements to ensure that the costs plus profit margins are guaranteed.

6 | Hire-purchase

Synopsis of service

Hire-purchase may be either:

(a) *lender credit*, whereby the customer buys the asset direct, borrowing funds himself from a finance house, or (more usually)

(b) *vendor credit:* involving a debtor-creditor-supplier agreement, whereby the vendor has a relationship with a finance house and affects an introduction to the purchaser or acts as their agent in agreeing a hire-purchase agreement. The finance house purchases the asset, then collects the hire-purchase instalments from the customer. Strictly title passes at the end of the hire period, but depending on the terms of the credit sale agreement, the customer may obtain title at the outset. The agreement will also set out any deposit requirements, and prevailing government restrictions.

Also split into:

(a) *consumer hire-purchase* for personal individuals and regulated by the Consumer Credit Act 1974 for loans up to £15,000—usually provided at the point of sale in the form of vendor credit, and

(b) *industrial hire-purchase* for corporate entities. Often referred to as lease purchase, industrial hire-purchase is similar to leasing except that the customer inherits title at the end of the agreement.

Suitable cases

Consumer hire-purchase

Any personal customer wishing to purchase any fixed asset over a term, as an alternative to bank finance, which will not necessarily be available at the point of sale.

Industrial hire-purchase

Any corporate wishing to purchase a fixed asset over a term without using bank finance, but wishing to obtain title either at the outset or ultimately, which has the capacity to benefit fully from writing-down allowances through an adequate profit stream.

Marketing benefits

Small, or no, capital outlay required.

Customer retains full ownership of asset at the end of the agreement.

Regular monthly repayment terms over a specified period assist with accurate cash-flow forecasting.

For personal customers, the ability to spread payments through a hire-puchase agreement frequently enables the purchase of an asset which otherwise would not have been possible.

Capital allowances are available providing the company has sufficient taxable profits.

Relatively simple to arrange—usually available at the point of sale removing the need to negotiate 'outside' finance.

Costs

Historically more expensive than bank finance, due to the higher risk, lack of branch record etc., but more recently interest-free or beneficial terms are commonplace as an inducement to purchase specific items. In such situations, however, it may be cheaper to negotiate discounts and fund from traditional bank finance (particularly in the case of new cars).

Usually the inherent rate will be fixed, but variable rates linked to finance house base rate, and the money market are common for industrial hire-purchase.

7 | Mortgage Finance

Synopsis of service

Traditionally the product of building societies, mortgages are now increasingly available from banks to new and existing customers. Levels of loans will differ from one organisation to another but generally 3 to $3\frac{1}{2}$ × gross salary plus 1 × secondary income will be available, up to 90% of purchase price or valuation or up to 100% with a mortgage guarantee. Age, condition, type of property and amount sought will all affect the conditions of the mortgage agreement.

In a *straight repayment* mortgage, monthly interest and capital repayments ensure full repayment over a specific term.

With *endowment-linked repayment*, interest only is covered monthly with capital repaid in full from the proceeds of an endowment policy on maturity, usually aged 65, or on earlier retirement.

A *pension-linked* mortgage is a similar arrangement to an endowment mortgage but, by using a personal pension plan, tax advantages no longer available for endowment policies following the Finance Act 1984 can still be obtained.

Bridging loans and structured home-improvement loans complement the different types of mortgages to provide a full house-financing package.

Suitable cases

All existing or potential houseowners usually from socio-economic groups C1 and above, considering properties in the UK for owner occupation as a main residence—although schemes also exist for holiday homes.

Quotations for all types of mortgage should be sought to assess the most appropriate.

'Pension mortgages' will suit those in a position to tie in a pension option—self-employed or those with existing personal pensions.

Corporate schemes, specifically constructed for individual companies with executives and employees involved in frequent relocation. Such schemes will generally involve both bridging and mortgage finance, often with background company support to cover any losses.

Marketing benefits

Enables purchasers to obtain ownership of property at a monthly cost, similar to a rental charge.

Provides an excellent investment opportunity.

Tax relief at standard rate is available on interest payable on mortgages of up to £30,000.

Endowment option provides life cover for the currency of the loan and, depending on the terms and performance of the assurance society, will usually provide a lump sum on maturity after repayment of the loan capital. Policies taken out prior to 14 March 1984 attract tax relief at 15%.

Pension mortgages provide a pension option, which attracts full tax relief, both on capital and interest.

Use of 'bank' mortgages additionally provides a quick and efficient service at competitive rates with immediate availability of funds on assessment (building society mortgages often involve a delay if deposits are low).

A full related service—insurance, personal loans for furnishings etc.—is provided by the banks.

Costs

Arrangement fee—varies from lender to lender but usually £100 to £200 as a flat fee.

Inspection or survey fee—calculated on a scale approximately 0.1% of the valuation.

Legal costs—usually calculated on a scale of 1% plus stamp duty and any other disbursements, plus bank security costs.

Interest—varies: usually it is charged at an issued mortgage rate, which is generally 1–2% above base rate.

Banks' interest is sometimes calculated on an annualised basis, whilst building society loans are serviced on the balance at the beginning of the year. The differential can equate to up to 1% difference in APR.

8 | Farming Finance

Synopsis of service

Financial

Generally needs fall into three areas:

(a) Working capital to cover seasonal fluctuations in cash flow, generally the purchase of seeds, fertilisers and foodstuffs ahead of harvest proceeds, or, in the case of dairy farmers, the milk cheque. Standard overdrafts are appropriate for such a need.

(b) Short-term finance for the purchase of machinery and vehicles. Repayment will normally be geared over the useful life of the asset and funded from cash flow. Farm development loans provide fixed-rate structured facilities, whilst a variable-rate loan could also be applied. Hire-purchase and leasing are alternative ways of funding with the opportunity to incorporate a servicing option on an 'operating lease' package.

(c) Longer-term finance generally to fund the purchase of a farm. Increasingly the banks are becoming involved with such financing, but traditionally this has been the market for such bodies as the Agricultural Mortgage Corporation (AMC).

Advisory services

Most banks have a specialist farming unit able to offer advice. These units are, however, staffed largely by bankers and the concentration is therefore on financial advice and budgeting. More technical guidance is available from bodies such as the National Farmers Union (NFU) for advice on costs and prices, the Agricultural Development and Advisory Service (ADAS) and the Meat and Livestock Commission.

Suitable cases

Literally every farmer is a potential target with the ongoing need for constant replacement of machinery and opportunities to expand farms through the purchase of adjacent acreage.

Marketing benefits

The specialism available from banks' agricultural units enables farmers' propositions to be viewed in a realistic light. There is an appreciation of seasonality which may extend over a considerable period in the event of a failed harvest.

Constant liaison with numerous different farming customers helps the unit build up a bank of relevant information for particular farming sectors against which individual farmers can assess their performance and implement schemes which have proved successful elsewhere.

The provision of Farm Development Loans enables a farmer to fix his funding expenditure in the knowledge that it will not fluctuate from month to month. This will assist in cashflow management.

Costs

Advice to farmers is generally free on the basis that spin-off business in the form of loans, leasing etc. will result.

Margins for farm lending are usually quite fine, against the extensive land security which is frequently available. A rate of 1% + base rate would be realistic for variable-rate borrowing. Structured-rate borrowing would be at the prevailing market rate on agreement of the facility.

9 | Franchising

Synopsis of service

'Business format franchising' is an arrangement whereby a self-employed person is able to operate his own business using the service and experience of a previously market-tested business. Typical examples would be fast-food chains, car exhaust or fashion retail outlets, e.g., MacDonalds, Tie Rack, Kwik Fit.

The franchisor is the company or individual which has market tested, and owns the copyright of, the business.

The franchisee is the new entity wishing to purchase a franchise to operate in the name of the proven business, and receiving advice and guidance from the franchisor. The franchisor will usually be a member of the British Franchise Association which lays down a strict code of conduct.

Services from banks are:

(a) Advisory:

(i) Advice on constitution of the franchise contract, comprising both the purchase agreement and the franchise agreement, setting out the conditions of the franchise, royalties etc.

(ii) Advice on the evaluation of a franchise, the likelihood of service, and potential level of profitability.

(iii) Details on the standing of an existing franchisor.

(b) Financial:

(i) Usually to the franchisee, in the form of setting-up capital, often a structured business development loan.

(ii) Also in the provision of working capital by way of overdraft.

Suitable cases

Potential franchisees—individuals interested in self-employment via a franchise.

Potential franchisors—individuals or companies with a proven track record who see the opportunities for expansion but do not wish to extend their own responsibilities.

Existing franchisors who wish to expand their franchise network.

Marketing benefits

Franchisor

Ability to widen catchment area for product.

Increase income, through royalties, without investing further capital.

Likelihood of commitment from franchisees, with their own investments at stake.

Franchisee

Opportunity to start business, but with a proven track record— increased likelihood of business in early vulnerable months.

Training and advice on business and selection of site available from franchisor. Advertising and personnel assistance also available.

Equipment and raw materials supplied direct from franchisor, thus simplifying purchasing processes (although opportunities for economies are removed).

As a downside of independence—to some degree success will depend upon the success of other franchisees' operations.

Costs

Advice is usually provided free of charge.

Borrowing costs will be in line with the type of loan or overdraft.

10 | Factoring and Invoice Discounting

Synopsis of service

Factoring

(a)   Debtor administration. The factoring company will:

- (i)   Monitor and maintain the sales ledger.
- (ii)   Issue and dispatch invoices.
- (iii)   Collect debts on due dates.

(b)   Credit protection. The factor offers a 'without-recourse' service which guarantees settlement of all trade debts. Additionally, undertakes credit reference enquiries.

(c)   Advances against debtors (optional). Provision of up to 80% without-recourse finance of trade book debts on issue of invoice. Percentage advanced depends upon type of business, strength of company, and quality of debtors. A charge over book debts will be taken.

Invoice discounting

Discounting of specific invoices to provide immediate finance. Facility is with recourse and the company retains full control of debtor invoicing, and collection.

Suitable cases

Factoring

Non-specialist companies with growth and profit potential, and annual sales turnover in excess of £100,000. Sound balance sheet and management.

Often lacking in administrative control and debtor control and collection systems, with sizeable amount of working capital tied up in debtors.

Well spread debtor portfolio, average invoice in excess of £75 (export factoring £200), average credit period less than 90 days (export factoring 20 days).

Reasonable bad debt record (unless the result of poor management).

Invoice discounting

Largely as for factoring but minimum turnover of £500,000, several large debtors and emphasis on need to improve cash flow rather than control debtor collection.

Marketing benefits

Factoring

Debt administration. Computerised sales ledger administration will provide improved quality and efficiency of service at reasonable price.

Efficient and prompt collection of debts will result from professional expertise of factor, enabling improved cash flow and opportunities for increased productivity.

Staff savings—reduction in administrative staff, and release of management time to concentrate on sales and marketing.

Credit protection. 100% protection against bad debts on approved sales will improve both profitability and cash flow.

Provision of credit intelligence will improve market awareness and risk assessment.

Advances against debtors. Increased cash available allowing early settlement of creditors to obtain discounts, or increased productivity.

Seasonal peaks can be financed without need to raise further borrowings.

Factoring is 'off balance sheet' and, therefore, permits raising of cash without affecting gearing.

Improves accuracy of cash-flow forecasting.

Invoice discounting

As with 'advances against debtors' above. Additionally, as the company retains control of the sales ledger, its customers are unaware of the arrangement.

Costs

Factoring

For debt administration and credit protection: service charge between $\frac{1}{2}$% and $2\frac{1}{2}$% of sales turnover plus VAT, dependent on risk, quality of customer and debts.

For advances against debtors: 2 to 4% over base rate (usually slightly higher than overdraft).

Invoice discounting

Commission charge $\frac{1}{4}$ to $\frac{3}{4}$% of sales turnover plus VAT.

Discount charge—expressed as percentage over base rate (usually slightly higher than overdraft).

11 | Cash Management

Synopsis of service

Cash management services have grown rapidly over recent years with the growing sophistication of companies and establishment of corporate treasury functions.

To facilitate the arrangement of cash, banks can supply a range of computer-based services from a simple balance reporting system whereby a company has a personal computer on which it can call up the balances of its subsidiaries, and the gross and net group position. From this base investment or funding decisions can be made.

Reporting of transactions on a daily basis is an option available, and a money transfer service enabling a company to transmit funds direct to beneficiaries, subject to certain security requirements, can be added.

At the more sophisticated end a company can install a full cash management package which affords:

(a) Current balance information on subsidiaries.
(b) Net balances within groups across several subsidiaries.
(c) An overall concentration account picture being the aggregate of all debit and all credit balances over all the companies' accounts.
(d) The ability to charge automatically a set interest rate at a level to suit the central treasury function—in some cases penal rates can be programmed. Any interest charges can then be levied to the credit of the central treasury of the corporate as central treasury will have carried the day-to-day funding costs for the group on a net basis.

The end result is the availability of an up-to-date extensive synopsis of the group's cash position, both on an individual subsidiary basis, and on net and gross group basis.

Suitable cases

Large to medium-sized corporates with more than one operating account. Companies with numerous subsidiaries are ideal targets.

Marketing benefits

The opportunity to set off debit balances on a group basis against available credit balances minimises borrowing costs, and maximises the effective use of the credits. Additionally, subject to the companies' agreement and the provision by the companies of letters of set-off across the accounts involved, the bank is permitted to 'pool' (i.e., set off) the credit and debit balances for Bank of England reporting purposes; by doing so mandatory liquid asset charges are reduced.

The interest apportionment to borrowing subsidiaries calculated on a daily basis, permits the central treasurer to force subsidiaries to manage their own borrowing costs and, in doing so, encourages them to reduce bank reliance. The spin-off effect in the group's gross and net positions is a reduced borrowing need and related funding cost savings.

Additionally the treasurer has a far more comprehensive base from which to make funding decisions and deposit surplus balances on a daily basis.

Costs

The cost will be very much dependent upon the depth of service taken. As a guide a simple balance reporting package will cost in the region of £200 per annum.

12 | Payroll Services

Synopsis of service

A system making use of the bank's computer to distribute a customer's payroll.

Payment can be made on a frequency to suit the employee:

    (a)   Direct into employees' accounts by BACS (Bankers Automated Clearing Service)—the most usual method today.
    (b)   Into employee's accounts by paper Bank Giro credits.
    (c)   By individual cheques or by cash in pay packets—although cash payment is now uncommon.

To support each payment method employers are provided with listing and annual tax returns.

Alterations can be accommodated immediately—pay details are produced on an exceptional basis—i.e., previous details run automatically in the absence of amendments.

The debit to the employer's account is deferred to coincide with the day of payment to the employees.

The partial repeal of the Truck Acts enables a more extensive use of computerised pay systems.

Suitable cases

Businesses with large debtor/creditor pay lists; any employer with in excess of 10 employees is a likely user.

Companies with bulk manual entries or users of large volumes of cheques should be encouraged to explore payroll.

Any business with a stretched administration function or considering changing its administration arrangements could benefit.

Marketing benefits

Employees

Provision of a bank account will assist budgeting and offer a convenient means of saving.

Increased security with removal of cash carrying.

Employers

Reduced workload, and consequent savings.

Possibility of saving two days' interest costs.

Substantial savings as security costs are minimised.

Potential staff savings.

Flexibility—many schemes are available with options to suit specific needs.

Improved cash flow from the opportunity to switch weekly paid employees to monthly pay.

Frequently the involvement of unions will be necessary to introduce any changes in methods of pay and consideration will need to be given to appropriate marketing. Free banking for employees for a specified period may be an acceptable incentive.

Costs

Will vary from scheme to scheme and will take into account volumes involved and specific requirements of the employee. A quotation is usually given only once the amount of work involved is known.

13 | Credit and Charge Cards

Synopsis of service

Cards are considered either as 'credit' or 'charge' cards. With credit cards there is a requirement to clear at least part of the outstanding balance on a monthly basis, with the balance being subject to a published interest rate. Charge cards require repayment of the full balance on a monthly basis. They do not provide credit facilities.

As a complementary service, most credit card companies now offer fixed loan facilities to run alongside the credit card facility.

Banks can provide credit and finance lines to large corporates, such as chain stores, who wish to run their own scheme, usually at substantially higher rates from the borrowing cost. Alternatively the credit card company can act as the corporates' agent and run schemes on their behalf and generally in their name.

Increasingly companies are using corporate schemes for their own employees' expenses. Under such an arrangement cards would be issued to participating employees in their own names to be used ostensibly as their own cards. The bills, however, are sent direct to the employer.

The most common arrangement remains personal cards which are accepted at outlets which have entered into a 'merchants' agreement' whereby a floor limit for maximum amount acceptances is set. Against the payment of a negotiated commission fee, the credit card company guarantees payment.

Most credit card companies also provide 'gold' cards for premium customers. Such arrangements provide overdrafts (up to £10,000) at preferential rates in addition to a package of other benefits. High income earners (£20,000 p.a.) or high asset owners (£100,000 plus) are target customers.

Suitable cases

All individuals with regular incomes.

Companies with employees on expenses.

Virtually all shops—but particularly those selling consumer durables.

Shops looking to increase sales.

Marketing benefits

Merchants

Payment guaranteed and convenient—increasingly so with the intro-duction of 'swipe systems'.

Funding cost savings—credit card payments treated as cleared moneys when paid in.

Increased sales—attraction to customers by paying by credit; mail order system allows payment by telephone.

Mail shot opportunities through the credit card company.

Employers for expenses arrangement

Reduces petty cash.

Aids budgetary control.

Reduces administrative burden—one statement for each employee.

Monthly payment may improve cash flow.

Maintains tighter control on employees claiming expenses.

Facility is of a revolving nature.

Individuals

Reduces need to carry cash—also provides purchasing power without the need to plan.

Provision of credit without the need to seek prior bank approval. Enables repayment programme to match card owners' specific finances.

Free credit up to a specified period available.

Cash withdrawals available through participating banks' automated teller machines.

Ability to join the credit card company in an action against the supplier of goods.

Costs

Merchants

Will pay a flat percentage fee per transaction. This is negotiable when the initial arrangement is agreed and will be between 1% and 5%.

Expenses employers

Subject to negotiation between the employer and the credit card company, but usually set at a flat charge per employee.

Individuals

A charge card will be provided subject to an annual membership fee, usually around £30 p.a.

A credit card is provided free, with interest charged on outstanding balances not cleared within a specified period (usually between 25 and 40 days depending on schemes). Interest is generally set at around 2% per month (APR 26.8% p.a.), but in-house schemes run by chain stores are frequently more expensive.

14 | Electronic Money Transfer

Synopsis of service

Over recent years CHAPS has become established as the most recognised method of electronic transfer of funds. This is an electronic network between the major English and Scottish clearing banks enabling transfers to be made either through the banks or through direct access from accepted corporate customers with their own terminals. For such customers the bank would put in place a daily limit. Certain refinements to the system are available enabling the user to extract a summary of payments in and out during the day to allow for end-of-day balance proportions and appropriate funding/investment action.

EFTPOS (electronic funds transfer at point of sale) is a major electronic development. This is a scheme whereby the retailer debits a customer's account directly through the use of a magnetically encoded plastic card. At the time of purchase one card is 'wiped' through the retailer's terminal which is on-line with the bank's computer. The customer authenticates the payment by keying in his PIN (personal identification number). If the computer authorises the transaction the customer's account is debited (usually immediately) and the retailer credited. The system is largely experimental—Barclays has introduced its 'Connect' card, and National Westminster its 'Switch' card, but the overall concept has yet to be widely accepted.

Service tills (or cash dispensing machines) and automatic deposit machines are a further breakthrough into electronic banking. These provide 24-hour banking enabling customers to obtain cash by way of a personally encoded magnetic plastic card, with a PIN, through hole-in-the-wall machines.

Suitable cases

Personal customers are the principal target sector for all plastic banking—this is a major way for banks to cut costs by paper removal. Clearly creditworthiness is a factor.

The use of the CHAPS system is particularly relevant for corporates and professionals (especially solicitors) who have a need to transfer sizeable amounts with same-day value.

EFTPOS is a service ideally suited to chain stores and garages with a high volume of relatively small payments.

Marketing benefits

CHAPS

Total security is ensured as all payments are made through British Telecom's 'packet switching' service (PSS). This effectively breaks down the message and can be further enhanced by scrambling.

Guaranteed same-day value with associated cash-flow benefits.

Cost savings and convenience as paper is removed from the system.

EFTPOS

Convenience, removal of paper and speed avoiding queuing.

Cost savings.

Same-day value enhances cash flow.

Costs

The use of the CHAPS system involves fixed costs, which together with a margin will be passed on to the customer. The fee per payment will be in the region of £12 to £15.

As EFTPOS is still in its early stages there is no real accepted basis for charging, but it must be accepted that to replace paper, the related charges must demonstrate some form of saving. As such it would be realistic to consider a charging basis lower than the cost of a cheque.

Cards such as cash dispenser cards are provided free of charge.

Executor and Trustee Services

Synopsis of service

Banks offer a range of executor and trustee services revolving around making a will and administering an estate. The marketing emphasis in making a will is to avoid the restrictive conditions of an intestate estate.

The bank can offer advice and act in the drawing up of the will.

The bank is named either as primary executor, or secondary executor in the event of the named executor having died or being unwilling to act.

Under the will the bank's responsibilities will include:

(a) Obtaining probate and dealing with the estate as appointed.
(b) Handling funeral arrangements.
(c) Agreeing the estate value with the taxation authorities, and paying the death duties.
(d) Payment of all other debts and expenses.
(e) Collection and liquidation of assets.
(f) Distribution to the beneficiaries on settlement of the estate.

A related service is that of estate management whereby advice is given to minimise the level of inheritance tax on death. This is levied at 40% for estates in excess of £118,000. The emphasis is on drawing up a will in the most effective way, the restructuring of an estate to make use of available IT exemptions, and the use of life assurance to cover forecast IT liabilities.

Suitable cases

Simply anyone with a sizeable estate and no will. Ideal occasions for marketing wills are:

(a) Marriages.
(b) Birth of a child.
(c) Holidays, or overseas travel.
(d) Change in personal circumstances (divorces).

(f)   Maturity of a life policy.
(g)   Recent windfall or inheritance.
(h)   Retirement.

Marketing benefits

The bank's advice is impartial and trustworthy. Experience of the trustee department ensures a professional approach.

Continuity is assured—whereas a specific executor may have deceased—notwithstanding the period of the trustee duties.

Secrecy is assured and family disputes avoided.

The burden of administration of a will, which is frequently distressing, is passed to the bank.

Taxation is minimised under professional advice.

Costs

This will vary from organisation to organisation—but a basic fee for a will handling will range from 5% to 2% on the value of the estate. The charge for estate management will reflect the volume of work involved.

16 Taxation Advice

Synopsis of service

All areas of tax are advised upon across personal, business and trust situations.

Personal advice covers:

(a) Handling of income tax claims.
(b) Computation of capital gains tax claims.
(c) Effective use of allowances.
(d) Preparation of tax statements for grant and rent purposes.
(e) Completion of annual tax return, and handling tax vouchers, dividends etc.

See also part B, chapter 15 on estate planning.

Business advice covers:

(a) Provision of specialist guidance on effective use of taxation, use of leasing etc.
(b) Preparation of accounts for submission to the Inspector of Taxes.

Suitable cases

Individuals with complex tax situations:

(a) High-salary earners.
(b) Expatriates.
(c) Widows and elderly customers with dividend income.
(d) Substantial income earners.
(e) Receivers of gross income.
(f) Small businesses or self-employed customers without access to their own tax advisers and accountants.

Marketing benefits

Assurance of accurate assessment of tax, avoiding subsequent claims for unpaid tax, or initial overpayments.

Removal of time-consuming administration in handling tax returns, dividend vouchers etc.

Professional expert advice with access to relevant taxation offices to negotiate disputes or handle queries.

Provision of comprehensive advice for those living abroad.

Extension of the cradle-to-grave concept.

Costs

Will depend upon the extent of service, whether simple advice, or a full service of administering all tax affairs, completing tax returns and negotiating with the Revenue. Frequently, however, the cost is considered as worthwhile expenditure to compensate for the removal of the administrative and financial headaches associated with running one's own taxation affairs.

17 | Pensions

Synopsis of service

As personal pensions plans become more common with the option of employees to opt out of corporate pension schemes there are three major ways in which banks can assist with customers' pension needs:

(a) *Insured corporate schemes*, in which payments are made by a company into an insurance policy by way of premiums. These represent monthly deductions from, or payments on behalf of employees with associated tax benefits. The insurance company involved underwrites the value of the scheme offering a guaranteed minimum pension and usually integral life assurance to cover death prior to retirement. The bank's insurance subsidiary would act as broker in identifying the most cost-effective and appropriate scheme.

(b) *Managed-pension funds*, where the bank can act as trustee of a fund managed directly by the corporate employer on behalf of the employees to ensure the rules of the fund are adhered to and the interests of the employees are preserved. Alternatively the bank's subsidiary can undertake a full manager role whereby it invests in chosen investments, either on an indexation, income, or capital growth basis to provide future pension income. Again, the company makes monthly payments into the fund on behalf of the employees.

(c) *Personal pension plans*, in which the bank's subsidiary (or an insurance company) will administer a personal fund on behalf of an individual, and invest on his or her behalf in accordance with a defined strategy. This plan continues as the individual moves from employer to employer without loss.

Suitable cases

Companies whose administrative function is unable—either through lack of capacity or lack of experience—to handle an in-house scheme. Having identified an appropriate target presentations will be given by the pension subsidiary to identify whether an insured scheme, or managed scheme is more appropriate.

Professional individuals who tend to move from employer to employer or high earners who wish to invest heavily in a pension plan with a view to early retirement.

Self-employed individuals with no existing pension arrangements, who will, on retirement, otherwise have recourse only to a State pension.

Marketing benefits

Corporates

Experience both in handling the administration of pension schemes and in effective investment of funds.

Wide experience in identifying the most profitable insurance company schemes based on past track record.

Contributions are tax allowable.

Potential for release of staff and consequent cost savings.

Impartiality of banks, as opposed to possible criticism of parochial investment by in-house schemes.

Encouragement of employee loyalty.

Individuals

Tax-efficient investment for the future—provision for the family.

For self-employed schemes the individual has the flexibility to move from employer to employer without loss of benefits.

Professionalism of bank's administration, and tax benefits provide a return usually greater than the potential for growth from personal investments.

Costs

Will depend upon the extent of the service to be provided and the volume. Additionally the extent of investments to be made will have an impact. As a guide, however, a modest personal pension plan administration would cost in the region of 1 to 2.5% p.a. of portfolio value.

18 Investment and Savings Schemes

Synopsis of service

To recognise the increased sophistication of customers an extensive range of savings schemes are available. Additionally banks provide a full investment management service.

Savings schemes

On demand—simple deposit account providing a relatively low rate of interest, but allows immediate withdrawal. Some schemes also provide a cheque-book facility.

Term deposit in investments requiring a period of notice to be given prior to withdrawal, pays a higher rate of interest than 'on demand'.

Premium deposits—involving higher amounts (some schemes also require withdrawal notice, or permit only one drawing per annum). A premium rate of interest is paid.

Money market deposits—investment directly into the money market for a fixed term, which will attract a fine rate in line with market conditions. The interest rate will be fixed.

Offshore deposits—investments outside the UK tax authorities and as such not subject to UK tax.

Investment management schemes

The management by the bank on an ongoing basis of a customer's investment portfolio. Normally only portfolios in excess of £10,000 are accepted. Customers can specify the type of investments made, whether any particular sector of shares should be favoured or avoided. The scheme can be either *discretionary* where the bank has full authority to buy and sell as it sees fit, or *non-discretionary* whereby the customer's authority is sought prior to any investment change.

In either case the bank handles rights and bonus issues, and, if required, tax management can be added.

Suitable cases

Savings

Both personal and corporate customers who are cash rich or have a regular savings need.

Investment management

High net worth individuals, busy executives without the time to manage their own investments, or those located abroad who are out of touch with the market. Retired customers who wish to avoid the administration and worry of running their own investment portfolio are likely targets.

Marketing benefits

Savings schemes

Whilst interest on regular bank schemes is paid on a net-of-tax basis (composite-rate tax paid), the rates are competitive in the bank market, although do not usually match building society rates.

Security is, however, virtually guaranteed.

Money market investments and offshore deposits will frequently carry interest rates greater than building societies, as interest is generally paid gross. Interest on the offshore schemes is not disclosed to the UK tax authorities.

Investment management

Professional investment by experts on a day-to-day basis.

Removal of administrative worry and concern at wrong personal investment decisions through lack of experience.

Avoids risk of missing rights and bonus issues.

Enables an investment portfolio to be kept in line with current investment trends notwithstanding the absence of the beneficiary.

Costs

Savings schemes are run free of cost—the bank being satisfied with the endowment effect of the saved moneys for its income.

Investment management fees will depend upon the extent of service required but for a basic scheme around 0.75% annually on the value of the portfolio will be charged.

International Services— Personal

19

Synopsis of service

Financial

Subject to the usual credit considerations banks are able to provide borrowings in the major foreign currencies. Most frequently such borrowing relates to mortgages for overseas properties. Due to differing legal systems it is usual to rely upon equity in the UK property for security. Often the chosen path for such transactions is, however, through sterling borrowing, with payment for the property at the spot rates. This removes any ongoing exchange risk.

Transmission

Currency accounts, operating on a similar basis as standard sterling accounts are available for customers with dealings in foreign currencies. Transfers of funds can be effected by way of drafts, mail transfers, or telephonic transfers. The costs relating to drafts and mail transfers are similar. Telephonic transfers are more expensive, but the service far quicker.

Advisory

The banks' international networks enable them to maintain extensive information bases covering trade opportunities, country risk, exchange control regulations and suchlike. Additionally banks offer advice on travel needs, visas, currencies and can obtain passports on behalf of customers.

Travel

Provision of foreign currency, and travellers cheques (in sterling or currency), together with eurocheque cards and credit cards enable banks to offer a full service to customers about to travel. Additionally travel insurance, for both property and health can be handled through the banks' insurance departments.

Suitable cases

All personal customers either due to go on holiday or on business travel. Additionally high net worth individuals with aspirations for owning overseas property—either privately or through overseas time-share schemes. (UK schemes will require payment in sterling.)

Regular travellers to specific areas frequently run currency accounts rather than buying and selling travel facilities on each occasion.

Marketing benefits

The banks' expertise and long-standing business relationships in overseas locations provide a recognised source of reliable information.

Dealings in most currencies enables banks to make markets and undertake the provision of finance and travel facilities at competitive rates.

Reliance on the bank for all foreign needs removes the administrative burden from the individual, who in all likelihood will be thoroughly inexperienced in all areas.

The extensive correspondent bank relationships provide local contacts to handle any specific needs in overseas currencies.

Costs

In general, advisory services are provided free of charge. Standard tariff charges for drafts, mail and telephonic transfers vary between £10 and £50 depending upon the amounts involved. Similarly the cost of travel facilities will vary from bank to bank.

Borrowings in foreign currencies will be extended at similar margins to UK funding, but local 'base rates' (or costs of funds) will have a material effect on the end cost.

20 | International Services— Corporate

Synopsis of service

Financial

Various options are available from currency borrowing on a standard working capital basis, to the provision of produce loans for specific contracts.

Discounting overseas bills is a further way of raising working capital as is factoring (see part B, chapter 10) and forfaiting. This involves the purchase of the bills of exchange under the invoice at a discount, and the operation is little different from invoice discounting.

Trade requirements

The emphasis here is usually the collection of funds. The use of documentary collections and settlement on open account are typical methods, although the security of an irrevocable documentary credit provides guaranteed payment subject to specified documents being in order. Such arrangements do, however, require the presence of a bank as a 'conduit'. The bank will usually be asked to advise or confirm the credit. Advising is merely a notification role, whereas confirming (for a fee) ensures that the credit will be paid if for any reason the opening bank defaults.

A further way of adding security to the transaction is through the use of ECGD insurance cover, which can be effected through the bank.

In relation to overseas contracts there is a growing need for both interminable and terminable indemnities for such things as performance and tender bonds whereby the bank is effectively asked to underwrite the creditworthiness of a customer for a set amount of a contract.

Transmission

As with personal customers, currency accounts can be offered, transfers can be effected through drafts, mail or telephonic transfers; foreign cheques can be collected or negotiated, whereby the customer receives the funds relating to the cheque immediately. The conversion rate used includes a loading for the bank's funding costs, and in some cases banks reserve the right to impose an interest charge if the proceeds of the cheque prove difficult to obtain.

A few corporates make use of the London US$ clearing system, through which cheques in US$ can be negotiated rapidly (usually two days).

Advisory

Most banks publish economic literature forecasting rates (both exchange and interest), market conditions and industry trends. Additionally some provide educational pamphlets on, for example, the operations of documentary credits.

These are supported by experts in their fields calling on customers to offer first-hand advice both to the immediate management and also to clerical employees.

Suitable cases

Any exporting customer—particularly those just starting to export.

Marketing benefits

The bank's expertise and extensive knowledge of overseas markets.

An extensive network of correspondent banks ensures that there is a local expert on hand to deal with any opportunities.

Competitive rates due to the bank's position in the major money market dealing area.

Provision of advisory points keeps the client up to date without having to leave the office.

Costs

Again, most advisory services are cost free. Standard rates are levied on draft, mail and telephone transfers. Overdraft borrowings would generally carry the same margin as the UK sterling borrowing. Documentary credit and documentary collection would be charged on a scale basis of around 0.02% p.a.

21 | Exchange Rate Management

Synopsis of service

To remove any risk of exchange rate loss from a contract involving either payment or receipt of foreign currency, a customer has the following alternatives:

(a)   A spot conversion for the amount of the invoice, on the invoice date, although there may be a small time lag and hence a period of risk.

(b)   A forward contract for a fixed amount at a fixed exchange rate to be effected at a predetermined date, ideally to coincide with the receipt or payment of the currency.

(c)   An option forward contract, whereby a customer enters into a contract either to buy or sell an amount of currency between two fixed dates, at a fixed exchange rate. Between the two dates the funds can be provided or drawn in tranches (part take-up/part delivery). The contract must be fulfilled, however, by the final date.

(d)   A currency option whereby a customer pays up-front commission for the ability (but not obligation) to buy or sell a fixed amount of currency at an agreed rate by a predetermined date. If the rate moves against the customer there is no obligation to complete the contract, but the commission fee is not returned.

(e)   The use of a currency account if flows of the specified currency are frequent both as debits and credits.

Suitable cases

Any corporate involved in importing and exporting where a movement in exchange rates could have an adverse effect on profit margins.

These arrangements are available equally to personal customers who wish to fix an exchange rate in advance of a particular event.

Marketing benefits

The ability to fix exchange rates enables an importer or exporter to forecast accurately his profit margins and establish prices for the on-sale of goods or services without the worry of possible margin erosion or losses.

The use of forward options provides some flexibility not available from straightforward contracts; for both of these the customer pays no fee, the bank's profit lying in the potential for favourable rate movements prior to the contract date (the bank takes the risk).

Currency options offer the greatest flexibility with no compulsion to complete. They provide the comfort of a bottom-line exchange rate. The rate established will reflect the commission fee payable. Fixing a rate in this way enables corporates to budget and forecast profits. They are able to benefit from favourable movements in that they can allow the option to lapse (although they must pay the fee) but are protected from any collapse in the currency.

Currency accounts enable the matching of currency receipts and payments, and remove both the risk and 'turn' on conversion.

Costs

Standard costs for the operation of currency accounts with charges for cheque issuance, although these can be negated by credit balances. The costs for forward or option contracts reflect the interest rate differential between the two currencies and any likely movement in exchange rates over the period involved. Similarly the cost of entering a currency option combines the likely exchange rate movement and the cost to the counterparty—usually the bank—for hedging against any potential loss if the customer chooses not to proceed with the transaction. The net amount is expressed as an up-front commission and will vary depending upon how much the rate for the option, chosen by the customer, is 'in' or 'out' of the money (i.e., is above or below the forecast market rate).

22 | Advisory Services

Synopsis of service

Advice on virtually every area of finance is available from banks with some more specialised than others—e.g., foreign services.

There are, however, two particular areas where advice is mainly concentrated: small business advice and merchant bank advice.

Small business advice

Through a bank's business advisory service, a representative will generally call on the customer to assess past and forecast trading patterns, current financial and management strengths and weaknesses and balance sheet and liquidity trends. He will generally provide a report of his findings offering whatever advice is appropriate to achieve an improved performance.

Assistance can be given in the compilation and use of management accounts, cash-flow forecasts etc.

A review of profitability performance will be undertaken and compared with industry norms.

Merchant bank advice

Aimed at the mid to large corporate market, services from a merchant bank comprise guidance on mergers and acquisitions and introducing potentially compatible parties, advice (and trading) on capital market products.

Stock market flotations are handled by merchant banks who may be involved in the full underwriting of a placing on the Stock Exchange whilst smaller concerns may look to the Unlisted Securities Market or the Third Market.

Suitable cases

Small businesses in their formative years are those most likely to require advice. Deteriorating balance sheet ratios, strained cash flow or slipping profit margins are all indicative of the need for guidance.

Conversely successful corporates are those most likely to require the advice of merchant banks. Often family owned concerns in need of equity capital for expansion, or looking to sell off a successful company in favour of retirement are suitable targets.

Public quoted companies without existing merchant bank connections should be approached.

Marketing benefits

Small business advice

The expertise of specially trained advisers enables a thorough professional review.

Appreciation of the management accounting techniques explained by the advisers should pay dividends in future as the business develops.

The involvement of the bank provides it with a greater understanding of the company and as a result facilitates the development of a closer relationship—which will offer further business opportunities in the future.

Merchant bank advice

Customers of merchant banks are assured of confidentiality when considering sensitive developments.

They have the benefit of an experienced and professional team who are constantly in touch with changes in the market.

Using a merchant bank successfully to float a company provides an equity investment, frequently necessary for a growth of the company's business. An added factor is the effect on gearing, which will improve notwithstanding the increased availability of funds.

The expertise and market awareness of those involved in the mergers and acquisitions environment offers the opportunity for successful business fits, with consequent growth prospects.

Costs

For existing customers, or the probability of spin-off business opportunities, the business advisory service would be provided free of charge. For a non customer a charge would generally be made, the amount depending upon the extent of work undertaken, but for a full review, report and ongoing consultation a fee of £1,000 plus would be justified.

For merchant bank services the cost will depend entirely upon the service provided. For a successful company sale or purchase a substantial fee would be payable, although notwithstanding all the preparatory work, if ultimately a prospect did not proceed no fee would be charged.

23 | Insurance Services

Synopsis of service

Personal

Most major clearing banks have subsidiaries which specialise in insurance broking. On a personal basis the principal types of insurance are:

(a) Asset insurance, e.g., house contents, building, car insurance.

(b) Life assurance:

(i) Whole life term assurance—whereby life cover for a specified term is provided, but with no return at maturity on survival. Frequently used for mortgage protection to obviate the need for a house sale on the death of the main income earner.

(ii) Endowment assurance—life cover over a defined period but providing a lump sum at maturity on survival. A 'with profits' option can be added which incorporates a further amount, based on the performance of the insurance company, at maturity.

(iii) Sickness or 'permanent health' cover to provide an income should illness or injury necessitate the policy holder ceasing work.

(c) Pension assurance—basically an endowment policy, the proceeds of which are invested in an annuity at maturity to provide a regular income on retirement.

Business

Similar services exist specifically tailored for the needs of businesses or corporates:

(a) Asset insurance to protect the company's assets and premises.

(b) Public and employee liability to cover against any claims arising from injury to the public or employees resulting from an incident deemed to be the responsibility of the company.

(c) Loss of profits to cover profits following a loss which is the subject of an insurance claim, e.g., fire or theft.

118

(d)   Key-man cover to provide a lump sum on the death of an individual material to the success of a business or partnership. The resultant funds can be used either to service the continuance of the business through buying in replacement expertise, or for providing financial support to the bereaved family.

(e)   Pension assurance structured to provide a pension income at retirement.

Suitable cases

Individuals at all stages of life, but life cover is especially important on changes in personal life-styles involving dependents—marriages, birth of children etc.

Similarly any corporate is a potential insurance user; small professional businesses are particular targets in that there is usually a reliance on one or two key individuals for whom life assurance is appropriate.

Marketing benefits

The banks' insurance subsidiaries are independent and able therefore to offer unbiased professional advice.

They have knowledge of and access to the whole market and are constantly in touch with developments.

The customer therefore benefits from a comprehensive quotation and competitive pricing.

The concept of both asset insurance and life assurance provides peace of mind and removal of hardship from dependents. Mortgage protection will provide preservation of a family home. In the case of businesses it can ensure their continuance on the death of a key individual.

As a means of saving, life assurance is an effective vehicle providing, under endowment policies, a tax-free lump sum. Additionally premiums paid in respect of pension plans qualify for tax relief.

Costs

These are entirely dependent upon the individual's circumstances, location and extent of cover required. Different insurance companies will have different schemes and pricing formulae.

24 | Branch Marketing Strategy

Whilst marketing strategies will change from bank to bank, even from individual to individual, the following represents a typical format.

(a) Assess locality, predominant socio-economic grouping and target market.

(b) Undertake:

S (strengths)
W (weaknesses)
O (opportunities)
T (threats)

analysis on branch capabilities.

(c) Review branch objectives and set business targets.

(d) Define marketing strategy considering marketing mix of:

Price
Product
Place
Promotion

Under each heading review individual objectives and strategies.

(e) Assess cost and potential income forecasts.

(f) Set programmes and define time-scales.

(g) Put in place monitoring procedures and validation controls.

(h) Introduce formal marketing.